Media Hypnosis in Advertising and Politics

Kenneth R. Graham, Ph.D.

TO THE MEMORY OF

EDGAR O. GRAHAM

(1936 – 2008)

"The conscious and intelligent manipulation of the organized habits and opinions of the masses is an important element in democratic society. Those who manipulate this unseen mechanism of society constitute an invisible government which is the true ruling power of our country."

Edward Bernays, *Propaganda*

Contents

Acknowledgements

This volume culminates a long history of study and practice in psychology and hypnosis. Though many years have passed I cannot overlook the debt I owe to my late mentors Dr. Ernest R. Hilgard and Dr. Martin T. Orne. Thanks go also to Dr. René Girard and the members of the Girard Group at Stanford University. Over the years many students and colleagues helped and advised me in my research especially Lawrence D. Greene, Lauren Marra Passante, Dr. Jeffrey Rudski, and the late Dr. George Gordon. I owe a special debt of gratitude to the Peninsula Library System of San Mateo County, California and to the Trexler Library at Muhlenberg College. Elina Tanaka designed the front cover. Whitney Michael provided invaluable help with design and editing. My son, Edgar-Award-winning author Dr. Mark Graham, and my daughter-in-law Fauzia Graham, helped me in innumerable ways over the years to focus and improve my manuscript, and my wife Michele forbore with good humor the ups and downs of my writing persona. The following individuals kindly read the manuscript to offer feedback and advice: John W. Carson, III; Cathy Newell-Jackson; Dr. Philip Secor; Bettina Whaley; and Dr. Wojciech Zalewski.

Preface

There has always been tension between the rulers and the ruled, the masters and the masses. It is the centrifugal pull of self-desire against the welfare of the larger society, the tether that holds human history together. For much of that history society at large was the concern of a governing class: kings or priests, who often viewed the masses, scrabbling for survival, with disdain. As long as the masses were tied to the land and easily subjugated the system remained more or less stable though far from just. Then, a few hundred years ago, things began to change. The invention of moveable type, mercantilism, the emergence of a middle class, and the beginnings of industrialism spawned political philosophies that proclaimed the rights of ordinary men and women. In North America these changes gave birth to a new nation whose growing pains could simply be pushed westward until they had to be resolved. In Europe they produced a bloodbath that saw aristocrats beheaded and left the bourgeoisie quaking. The question was could the power of the masses be controlled or was civilization to end in anarchy? It is a question that remains open. The harsh truth is that human beings are an unstable amalgam of altruism bonded to a base of vicious selfishness. The base, what author Carl Sagan called "the dragons of Eden," is what nature has given all vertebrates to survive as individuals and as a species. The altruism, annealed over eons of evolution, enables us to overcome our animal nature and live in caring social groups. The enormity and complexity of our current world is proof that it has worked. The existence of atomic weapons and the palpable danger that we will use them is proof that it has not.

Even in the allegedly egalitarian United States the wealthy and powerful never really trusted the masses. In the Constitutional Convention of 1781 Colonel George Mason of Virginia said that giving the ordinary citizen the right to vote would be like referring "a trial of colors to a blind man."[1] Similarly, George Washington proclaimed that "mankind when they are left to themselves, are unfit for their own government."[2] The Constitution is a compromise that recognizes these views. It allows each citizen the right to vote for President, for example, but even today reserves the final choice to the College of Electors. The electors, appointed by the state legislatures, are technically free to vote for anyone eligible to be President, even if that person was not on the ballot. Occasionally a so-called "faithless elector"[3] will do just that but in practice the electors vote for the candidates to whom they are pledged on the basis of the popular vote.

Throughout the 19th century political philosophers struggled to find a new formula that would allow altruism and anarchy to co-exist in an industrialized world. For Karl Marx the answer was to obviate selfishness by eliminating private property, in other words, to dissolve individual rights into the well-being of the greater society. That solution was anathema to wealthy and powerful interests in Western Europe and the United States where a new understanding of the masses emerged based on psychology rather than economics. A critical problem for those who championed democracy was the reality that common men and women sometimes transformed, like Dr. Jekyll becoming Mr. Hyde, into an unruly mob that committed heinous acts of violence. Examples readily at hand and in recent memory included the Reign of Terror that occurred in France at the onset of the French Revolution (1793-1794) and the insurrection of the Paris Commune in 1871.

French social psychologist Gabriel Tarde anchored his explanation of social behavior in the concept of imitation. For Tarde the son's imitation of the father was the primal phenomenon that lies at the root of social behavior, a phenomenon that was not based on force or cunning but upon prestige. Tarde compared it with hypnosis[4] and his theories directly influenced those of Sigmund Freud. Tarde's views were simplified and popularized by his younger contemporary Gustave Le Bon who believed that one who became part of a crowd lost his or her individuality to what Le Bon called the "crowd soul" which he believed was intellectually inferior to the individual and inherently malignant. Le Bon viewed the crowd's emergence as "a kind of hypnotic regression to a prehistoric mental state of mankind."[5] Le Bon's theories of crowd psychology contributed to fascist theories of leadership, such as Hitler's *Mein Kampf*, which emerged in the early 20th century, but it is the writings of Tarde that are most relevant today because they relate to the use of communications media to influence the masses. Le Bon focused on the destructive proclivities of crowds which by nature exist in a particular place. Tarde, asserted, on the other hand, that the media were creating a vastly powerful *public* that existed across geographical boundaries. The importance of the crowd, he said, was a thing of the past, because it was incapable of extension beyond a limited area, whereas the public could extend indefinitely and its life became more intense as it extended.[6] The question became how to shape and control it.

Answers emerged after World War I. The war resulted not only in terrible death and destruction but in political revolutions that swept away the imperial houses of Austria-Hungary, Germany and Russia and, in the latter case, led to the creation of the Soviet Union. The revolution did not spread westward, however, and to classical Marxists that was a bit of a puzzler because Marx had predicted that the most industrialized nations, such as Great Britain, would be the first to fall. Italian philosopher and Communist Party leader, Antonio Gramsci, explained why they had not. According to Gramsci the capitalist states had maintained their status because they had achieved what he called "cultural hegemony," that is, they succeeded in convincing the working classes, (the "public") that upper class values were the common sense values of everyone. In the United States that meant that notions of limited government and private property became everyone's American Dream. The cast of the television show *High School Musical 3* (2008) summed it up in the hit song "We're All in this Together" asserting that: "all our dreams have no limitations." That is, of course, nonsense but attractive nonsense to teenagers who are the primary viewers of television.

In the years following the Great War Gramsci's insight was put into effect by a new industry conceived to manipulate public desires for products and politicians. Its primary purpose was to define the American Dream in terms of material wealth. Its birth was signaled by the publication of the book *Public Opinion* by political columnist and foreign affairs analyst Walter Lippmann. In the book Lippmann argued strongly against freedom of thought and for the scientific control of public opinion and public behavior.

Lippmann's writings amplified doubts about democracy that had been voiced by the nation's founders. Democracy requires the average man and woman to be aware of and to understand the contemporary issues of their government and to know something about the individuals whom they have elected to decide the issues for them. This may have been possible in the early days of the republic, although it is doubtful that rural farmers even then fully grasped such issues as currency, banking, foreign trade and diplomacy. By the beginning of the 20th century, Lippmann believed, the United States had become so large and complex that meaningful participation in government by the average American was impossible. As one writer put it, "Average citizens are hardly expected to master particle physics or post-structuralism. Why should we expect them to understand the politics of Congress, much less that of the Middle East?"[7]

In his early career Lippmann was a prominent progressive intellectual, but his progressivism changed in the years approaching World War I. He began to see hostility toward big business, which fueled such muckraking magazines as *McClure's,* and *Everybody's* as a threat to the nation and as the beginning of social disintegration. He turned against the muckraking press in favor of the application of the "discipline of science" to democracy. In other words, Lippmann proposed abandoning democracy in favor of a system that would manage the behavior of average Americans by scientifically controlling the information to which they were exposed. Some of that information was political. During World War I Lippmann served as an advisor to President Wilson and supported the creation of the Committee on Public Information (CPI), America's propaganda machine. It was deemed necessary because many Americans considered the war to be Europe's business; the United States had stayed out of the war until 1917, its penultimate year; and a large percentage of Americans shared a German heritage. One of the most effective tools of the CPI was the use of "Four Minute Men," a group of 75,000 volunteers from all over the United States, leaders of their communities, who gave brief pro-war speeches during the intermission periods at movie theatres. Over the course of 18 months until the war ended they addressed more than 11 million people, a few hundred at a time.

Talks to live audiences were effective, but the new medium of radio was vastly more powerful. A few broadcasts took place in various countries before World War I. Charles D. Herrold, for example, established the United States' first broadcasting station in San Jose, California in 1909, but radio's explosive growth occurred after the war. Station KDKA in Pittsburgh, Pennsylvania, the first licensed commercial station, began broadcasting on November 2nd 1920. By 1924 there were 2.5 million radio sets in the United States and the number of licensed broadcasting stations had increased to more than 500. By 1930 the majority of American homes had radios and by 1950 that number had jumped to 98%. For the first time in history men and women separated by distance, background, and inclination became a mass audience. Today there are more than 10,000 commercial radio stations in the United States, almost every household owns at least one radio, and more than 95% of Americans over the age of 12 listen to radio on the average more than three hours per day. Once the mass audience was formed it could not be dissolved.

The power of radio was its ubiquity and constancy. Listeners heard the same voices repeating the same political and commercial messages over and over, day after day. As Stewart Ewen wrote in his book *PR!: A Social History of Spin*: "If, prior to the war (World War I), public relations had been fired up by the apparition of an aware discerning population – one that had vigorously influenced the boundaries of public discussion – the public was now being conceived as an unconscious organism, eminently susceptible to the mesmeric power of mass suggestion."[8]

This book presents the case that Ewen's reference to mesmerism, or as it is also called hypnosis, is neither a metaphor nor hyperbole. Through radio, and later television, the power of suggestion drew not hundreds or thousands but millions of listeners into conformity as a magnet lines up iron filings. It made Bernays' goal of the "conscious and intelligent manipulation of the organized habits and opinions of the masses" possible, and, as the world soon saw, the results could be terrifying and apocalyptic.

Radio, abetted by television after World War II, became the force behind two of the most powerful social movements of the 20th century: the emergence of Nazism in Germany during the 1930s and 1940s, and the creation of the post-war consumer economy in the United States. Each had wide-reaching consequences. Nazism was a nightmare that resulted in tens of millions of deaths and the destruction of much of Europe. Consumerism, on the other hand, seems more benign, the fulfillment of the American Dream. Author and environmentalist Bjørn Lomborg, for example, points out that it has given us more leisure time, greater security, more education, more amenities, higher incomes, more food, and a healthier and longer life than people have ever had before. This is, he says, "the fantastic story of mankind, and to call such a civilization 'dysfunctional' is quite simply immoral."[9]

There is, however, a down side. The public relations industry is largely devoted to convincing ordinary people that the fulfillment of the American Dream is found in such things as automobiles, cigarettes, and other consumer goods. It is an industry built on two solid psychological principles. One is *envy*, that is, that human beings imitate the actions and desires of those whom they look up to or, as Tarde phrased it, those who have prestige. From the earliest days of media advertising products have been associated with famous and admired people. Advertising, in other words, is not generally based on the inherent qualities of a product, such as its speed or durability, but on the prestige of owning it. An economic system built on envy, on goals that by design can never be reached, on desires that can never be fulfilled, is frustrating, psychologically unstable, and unhealthy. Evidence is there if we look for it in a significant increase in alcohol consumption per capita in the United States since 1950, when the post-War media boom began, compared to the previous 100 years; the massive, wholesale use of prescription drugs for anxiety and depression by the public, drugs which are now bought widely and easily over the internet; and an increase in the United States of psychologists and other counselors since 1950 of more than 2000%. Moreover, much of the advertising that fueled the consumer boom was targeted at children who are more suggestible than adults, as in the common pairing of popular movie characters and toys with fast-food meals. Aside from the ethics of manipulating children in this manner, one result has been the explosive growth of childhood obesity.

The second principle upon which the public relations industry is built is *suggestibility.* Humans have a natural tendency to comply with suggestions, such as "you should try this product," especially when the suggestions are given, again, by someone to whom they look up. Suggestions given in the right context can produce powerful changes in the way individuals think about and perceive things including products, but suggestion is less well understood by social psychologists than imitation because it has been most identified with hypnosis whose peculiar and misguided history has deflected the serious study of suggestibility and compliance in everyday settings. Most importantly, measurements of individual differences in suggestibility, conducted in the context of hypnosis, show that a significant fraction of any population is more suggestible than the rest. Approximately 20% of men and women are much more influenced by suggestions given in hypnosis than are others, and there is evidence that these differences hold up in everyday life outside of hypnosis. This fact, that suggestibility may act as a sort of catalyst, has not been much explored in media studies but it may have far reaching social implications. In the 1930s author and editor V. F. Calverton said: "Contemporary society, with its radio, newspapers, films, schools, and churches, all attuned to the minute to what is happening in their respective realms, is more subject to hypnotic compulsion than any society which has ever existed in the past."[10] That is what this book is about, what some people call mass hypnosis.

1. The Reality of Hypnosis

Most people are familiar with hypnosis even if they have not personally used it. A Google™ search of the word *hypnosis* produces almost 10 million links to various web sites, almost 2 million within the United States alone. A large number of people know someone who has undergone hypnosis, and virtually everyone has seen hypnosis depicted on television as many popular shows such as *NCIS* and *CSI* have used hypnotists in their stories. Thousands of qualified hypnotherapists help men and women all over the world to stop smoking, lose weight, reduce pain, and to solve other problems. Over the past half-century hypnosis has taken its place as a respected specialty within medical and psychological practice. It was approved for use by responsible professionals by the American Psychiatric Association in 1958, and it has been a division of the American Psychological Association since 1969.

Nevertheless, there remains a sinister aura about hypnosis that puts many people off. Despite assurance from hypnosis practitioners that it is perfectly safe, what people often see and hear about hypnosis seems to imply a frightening loss of individuality and self-control. They are not completely wrong. There are ways in which unscrupulous individuals can use hypnosis unethically, perhaps not with every hypnotized person, but with some.

I saw the potential dangers first hand at the very beginning of my career. I studied hypnosis at Stanford University where I had the honor to receive my Ph.D.

degree under Professor Ernest R. Hilgard, one of the preeminent hypnosis experts of the 20th century. My first duty at his laboratory was to test prospective subjects for their ability to respond to hypnotic suggestions using a test of hypnotic susceptibility. There were several versions of the test but the procedure was essentially the same for each. The subject sat in a comfortable recliner chair in a quiet room while the experimenter read standardized instructions for the person to relax and gradually to become hypnotized. After that he or she was asked to respond to about a dozen specific suggestions. They included relatively simple things such as to hold one's arm out straight and feel it become heavy, a suggestion that most individuals experienced with ease, to more difficult suggestions that were experienced by only a minority of people. Two of these were the suggestions to forget (have amnesia for) the events of the session following its conclusion and to respond to a so-called post-hypnotic suggestion, that is, one that was meant to be carried out after the experimenter said that the hypnosis was over. In our tests that usually meant for the subject to get up and change chairs upon the appropriate signal, usually a pencil tap, by the experimenter.

During my first week at the laboratory I had the good fortune to test a few very good subjects, that is, men and women who responded to all, or almost all, of the suggestions on the test. At the end of one session I asked the woman with whom I had been working if she thought that she had been hypnotized. She said that she did not think so, that she had been very relaxed, but that she remembered everything that had happened. In fact, in scoring the amnesia item I found that she had remembered virtually none of the specific suggestions

2

used during the test. I then asked her how she got into the chair in which she was seated. A few moments before, when I tapped my pencil, she had gotten up out of the recliner chair and switched to an office chair in the corner of the room. At this point she looked startled, and I could tell that she was frightened. She did not know how she got into the chair, and I could see her wondering what else had happened during the session that she did not remember. In keeping with our protocol I reassured her and went over the entire test with her discussing each of the items. She left in a good frame of mind a few dollars richer for her participation. I learned, for the first time in my experience, that there really is something to hypnosis. Is it possible that a hypnotist could use the media to create many, perhaps millions, of such individuals who would follow that person's suggestions without being fully aware of why they were doing so, perhaps even to commit heinous acts of violence?

To answer that question one must determine whether hypnosis can take place via the media; whether a hypnotized individual can be made to do something against his or her will; and whether hypnosis, as it is commonly understood, can be used with masses of people as opposed to individuals.

Hypnosis via radio and television

Let's consider the questions in order. Attempts to hypnotize over the radio began shortly after commercial radio was introduced with some success. The first recorded attempt took place in New York in July, 1923. A hypnotist named Joseph Dunninger spoke through the air from station WHN which was then located in Ridgewood, Long Island. His subject, Leslie B. Duncan, was at the offices of *Science and Invention* magazine in Manhattan, 10 miles away. According to witnesses Dunninger put Duncan into a "state of trance from which he could not be aroused by ordinary means." As a result of Dunninger's suggestions Duncan's body became so rigid that a man could sit on it while it was suspended between two chairs. A needle plunged into Duncan's arm elicited no sign of pain, and when it was withdrawn, "no blood whatsoever issued from Duncan's wound."[1]

In March, 1927 a hypnotist named Gerald Fitzgibbons declared that within two minutes of the beginning of his program over Westinghouse station WBZ in Boston, two subjects in Springfield, Massachusetts and three others in Boston would be completely under his control. He arranged for psychologists, physicians, and newspaper reporters to witness the tests and, in the case of the subjects in Springfield, to report the results back to the studio. The results were inconclusive. The experts who witnessed the demonstration in Boston were not convinced that hypnosis had taken place. The results in Springfield were more positive. The subjects were examined by two psychiatrists who found that one of them was trying very hard but was not really hypnotized whereas the other behaved "in a manner which, on the whole, was stamped with greater genuineness."[2]

Similar effects were found a few years later when television broadcasting began. The first broadcasts took place in London in 1936 but hypnosis did not appear on TV until after World War II, a decade later. In December, 1946 the British Broadcasting Company auditioned a hypnotist named Peter Casson on an internal studio network at its television headquarters in the Alexandra Palace. It was the BBC's policy to give potential programs a tryout to judge audience reaction before broadcasting them to the public. Four judges watched Casson's face on television as he soothingly intoned that they would go to sleep. The four of them did, as did the studio announcer and a BBC employee in another room who switched on a monitor. The sleeping judges, one of whom was snoring gently, were awakened by shaking. They later said that they could not consider putting Casson on television because he was so good that he might be dangerous. The network subsequently issued a statement that it would bar all performers in the future who might "exert hypnotic influence."[3]

The examples demonstrate that certain individuals may become hypnotized via the media. The problem with them is that the techniques the hypnotists used to obtain compliance with their suggestions, that is to "hypnotize" people, were obvious, cumbersome and implied that the hypnotist had a special power that needed special conditions to take effect. They required subjects to be in a particular place at a particular time, to sit still, and to acquiesce in becoming hypnotized. That is not what happened in Nazi Germany. Hitler's listeners may have been moved by what he said but there is no evidence that they believed they were being hypnotized. It is not what happens when we watch television commercials either. We do not fall into a trance when a commercial comes on and begin to chant: "I must go buy a hamburger." Even though people can be hypnotized over the radio or television, if the conditions described above are required for mass hypnosis, then it unlikely that it could ever occur. The question is, are the conditions described truly the essence of hypnosis?

Hypnosis and crime

The second question asked whether a hypnotized individual could be made to commit an act, perhaps a criminal act, against his or her will. When people think about hypnosis and crime they may think of fictional accounts such as the story of Svengali or the Manchurian Candidate. The evil hypnotist Svengali appeared in the 19th century novel *Trilby* by George du Maurier. In the book a young Parisian artist's model named Trilby is spurned in love by an English artist who returns to London. In her sadness Trilby, who cannot carry a tune, is befriended by the sinister musician Svengali who makes love to her, hypnotizes her, and turns her into a successful singer. Some years later, at a performance in London, she and the artist meet again and rekindle their love for one another. Overcome by sadness and jealousy Svengali dies during the performance and Trilby immediately loses her beautiful voice. She falls ill, is cared for by the artist, but realizes that she is near death. She begins to make a will, sees a portrait of Svengali among her things, and goes into a trance. Her singing voice returns and for one brief moment she again sings beautifully and then dies with Svengali's name on her lips.

The movie thriller *The Manchurian Candidate,* a product of anti-communist hysteria, was released on October 24, 1962 at the height of the Cuban Missile Crisis. In it an American soldier, Sergeant Raymond Shaw, and his squad are captured by the Communists during the Korean War and subjected to a form of brainwashing that involves hypnosis. Shaw, played by Laurence Harvey, is trained to be a dangerous assassin who will enter hypnosis whenever he sees a particular playing card, the queen of diamonds. His handlers produce the cue when desired by calling Raymond on the telephone and suggesting that he play solitaire. The film builds to a suspenseful ending as it becomes clear that Raymond was specially chosen long in advance to assassinate his step-father, an American Presidential candidate. The film's shocking conclusion became even more poignant when President John F. Kennedy was assassinated, under still mysterious circumstances, by a lone gunman one year later.

Such fictional examples make exciting entertainment but do they contain any core of reality? In fact, there are a handful of cases in which hypnosis has been implicated in the commission of a crime, but the outcomes are ambiguous and can be attributed as easily to other factors, such as a romantic relationship between the participants, as to hypnosis.

In 1894, for example, Thomas McDonald, who was in his twenties, shot and killed Thomas Patton near Patton's home in Winfield, Kansas. At his trial McDonald's lawyer claimed that McDonald had shot Patton while under the hypnotic influence of an older man named Anderson Gray, and that he was therefore neither legally nor morally responsible for the crime. McDonald worked for Gray and had been hypnotized by him. According to newspaper accounts Gray convinced McDonald to murder Patton by telling him that Patton had made disparaging remarks about McDonald's wife. Gray's reason for doing this was that Gray was involved in a fraudulent real estate transaction to which Patton was the only witness. The prosecution clearly established that McDonald ambushed Patton and shot him with a rifle, but the jury acquitted him. Gray was subsequently found guilty of Patton's first degree murder, even though he was not present at the scene of the crime, and the verdict was upheld by the Kansas Supreme Court.[4]

The outcome was as remarkable at the time as it sounds today. Commenting upon it to a reporter, a New

York state Superior Court judge said, "So far as I am able to learn there has never been such a case in this world, certainly none in this country." The newspaper account of the case, however, was later disputed. The judge who presided over the trial of both men claimed that the question of hypnotism was never raised or insisted upon in the evidence, arguments, or instructions to the jury. According to him the only time that hypnosis was mentioned was when defense counsel said to the jury that "we might almost say that Gray possessed a hypnotic power over McDonald." The judge reported that Gray's influence over McDonald was of a "more vulgar stamp than that of hypnotic suggestion," but he did not explain what he meant by that.[5]

Perhaps the most infamous case in which hypnosis was claimed as a murder defense was in the death of Lt. Colonel William Farber of Middletown, New Jersey in July, 1963. Colonel Farber and his wife Marjorie lived across the street from Drs. Carl and Carmela Coppolino, both physicians. Carl Coppolino and Marjorie Farber had an affair and plotted to kill Marjorie's husband. Coppolino gave Mrs. Farber a powerful relaxant drug called succinylcholine chloride and instructed her to inject it into her husband. She testified at Coppolino's trial that she could not bring herself to do it, but three days later she injected him with a small dose that put him to sleep. At noon the next day, she claimed, Dr. Coppolino came to their house and smothered Farber with a pillow while saying: "He's a hard one to kill. He's taking a long time to die."

For a while they got away with it. Dr. Coppolino got his wife to sign Farber's death certificate saying that he died of a heart attack, and the Coppolinos subsequently moved to Sarasota, Florida. Marjorie Farber did as well and actually moved into the house next door to the Coppolinos. Carmela Coppolino apparently remained unaware of the affair between them and within months she was dead too. Dr. Coppolino got a physician friend to certify that she had had a heart attack, but the cause again was succinylcholine chloride. Coppolino might have gotten away with a second murder, but he betrayed his lover by marrying another woman, Mary Gibson. Enraged, Marjorie Farber went to the police and told the whole story.[6]

At his trial in New Jersey Coppolino was defended by the celebrated attorney F. Lee Bailey. Marjorie Farber was, of course, the chief witness for the prosecution. Acknowledging that she might be incriminating herself, Mrs. Farber told of the plot to kill her husband and her role in it. She declared that she had been under a hypnotic trance at the time of her husband's death which had been induced by Dr. Coppolino, and that she was therefore not responsible for her actions. She said that she could not stop herself, that she was beyond her free will, as if a large magnet had been pulling on her. Bailey defended Coppolino by attacking Farber's credibility. He described her story as nothing more than a cruel hoax perpetrated by a jilted woman, and Coppolino was acquitted. He was subsequently tried in Florida in the death of his wife and convicted of murder in the second degree. He served 12 years in prison, was paroled and returned to his second wife Mary. Marjorie Farber was never indicted.

If mass hypnosis involves forcing individuals to perform acts against their will then the evidence is against it happening. If, on the other hand, a persuasive speaker uses emotion effectively to change another person's desires, or to alter the person's reference to reality, then suggestion and crime may be linked. It is unlikely that hypnosis in the traditional context could be used to make someone to commit an active crime, such as murder, against another person. It is more likely that hypnosis could be used by an unscrupulous hypnotist to commit a crime such as sexual abuse against a passive, hypnotized person. To the best of my knowledge there are no documented cases of such abuse, but I once testified in a case that came close.

A 15 year-old high school girl was visiting another girl one day after school at the friend's apartment. A man was there who knew the other girl's mother, but the mother was not present nor was anyone else home. The girl who was visiting had a black eye, she had been in a fight, and mentioned this to the man when he remarked on her injury. He said that he could help her to get rid of her pain. In fact the man was an industrial psychologist who practiced hypnosis. He began gently to massage her temples which caused her to become very relaxed and led, allegedly, to sexual intercourse. At some point in this encounter the friend ran out of the apartment and was joined later on the front step by the girl with the black eye. She appeared dazed but eventually concluded that she had been raped. When the other girl's mother returned home and heard the story she called the police and the man was arrested. Prior to the trial I was asked to interview the alleged victim, along with her mother and rape crisis counselor, to determine whether indeed she could be hypnotized. Aware of the implications of the case I administered to her an abbreviated test of hypnotic susceptibility in which I purposely tried to get her to respond in atypical ways that would have suggested malingering. Based on my experience of more than 20 years, at that point, testing the hypnotizability of hundreds and hundreds of subjects, I believed her to be totally genuine, and I so testified at the man's trial. The defense, of course, brought forth a hypnotist who testified that using hypnosis in that way was impossible. That, and irregularities in the physical evidence, led to the man being acquitted. I felt at the time, and still do, that it is quite possible that a highly susceptible young woman had been taken advantage of.

Once again, however, the traditional view of hypnosis, and the means by which it is induced, argue against any possibility of mass hypnosis, but is the traditional view correct? If the essence of hypnosis is not, in fact, a special power exerted by the hypnotist to induce a trance, natural or supernatural, or a state of sleep, then hypnosis might occur in a variety of persuasive contexts. Hypnosis as it is traditionally understood may be an artifact of historical mistakes in the understanding of a fascinating and somewhat mysterious ability. We have addressed two of the questions we raised earlier. Chapters 3, 4, and 5 are an extended answer to the third, but first we must clear up some misconceptions about hypnosis.

2. Neither Magnetism nor Sleep

For thousands of years human beings realized that men and women influenced by exhortation, chanting, prayer, or other factors could experience powerful changes in the way they perceived and thought about their world. Often associated with religion these changes might include hallucinations or "visions," deep zombie-like states, or the ablation of pain as in fire-walking. An important component of these experiences was the belief that they would occur when suggested by the social context, by religious faith, or by the urging of other people. The men and women who experienced such phenomena recognized them as distinctly different from events of ordinary life.

Hypnotists do not have special powers

A little more than two hundred years ago a Viennese physician named Franz Anton Mesmer (1734-1815) believed that he had discovered the scientific grounds for such events as well as a means for inducing them, but his discovery was a mistake that impeded an accurate understanding of what we now call hypnosis for more than a century. It convinced many people that hypnosis was either a force, like magnetism, that could only be induced by people with special power in their eyes or hands, or a state that resembled sleep-walking. Neither of these beliefs is true but remnants of them persist to the present day.

Mesmer's peaceful gravesite in Meersburg, Germany contains clues to where he went wrong. His grave marker is a triangular block of stone that stands about waist high. On the top in the center of the triangle is a magnetic compass, and on one side is carved the image of a pyramid familiar to every American. At its apex is an eye surrounded by rays of light, the all-seeing Eye of Providence, which appears on the back of every dollar bill. These two symbols on Mesmer's gravestone reveal why hypnosis remains unique among the various branches and therapies of psychology. Mesmer was a physician who believed that physical illnesses could be cured by magnetism. The compass on Mesmer's grave symbolizes his belief in the healing properties of magnets as a unifying force of nature, its needle pointing north as a result of magnetic fields generated by the Earth. He believed that magnetic waves affected biological tissue as well as inert substances and that human beings could exude a healing force that he called *animal magnetism*. He used this force to cure a variety of ailments and pains that we would today probably call psychosomatic. Mesmer believed that he had discovered a unique power that he was reluctant to share openly with others. As he put it: "I am one through whom the universal healing fluid becomes effective. These cosmic energies which can heal every disease, mitigate every pain, radiate from my hands and from my words."[1]

Mesmer was also a Freemason and that is why the all-seeing Eye of Providence, a Masonic symbol, appears on his gravestone. His discovery of animal magnetism and his practice of magnetic healing were in accord with, and shaped by, Masonic principles. Masonry affected the development of mesmerism in two ways. First, it anchored it in a tradition of mysticism and the occult quite different from the contemporary un   derstanding of other forces such as Newton's studies of gravitation and Franklin's experiments with electricity. At the time of Mesmer's notoriety the occult sciences were enjoying a golden age in France.[2] Fortune tellers, faith healers, and astrologers prospered in a philosophical atmosphere of Rosicrucians, Swedenborgians, alchemists, and theosophists.[3] Mesmerism was more a descendent of this tradition than it was of experimental science. Secondly, the societies that Mesmer eventually established to promulgate animal magnetism were organized and conducted along the lines of Masonic lodges. Meetings, initiation rites, and instruction courses involved a combination of occult science and Masonic ritual.[4]

Mesmer's interest in magnetism and his first magnets came from a Jesuit priest who was director of the Vienna Observatory and a believer in the healing properties of magnetism, an idea that dated back to the 15th century alchemist Paracelsus. What Mesmer did was to make magnetism the foundation of a theory of healing fluid based on cosmic energy. Mesmer believed that disease was caused by a distortion or misalignment of this energy that could be restored to its natural balance both by physical magnets and by the "animal magnetism" within his own body.

Mesmer's first patient was a 27-year-old woman, Francisca Osterlin, who suffered periodically from more than a dozen severe symptoms, including convulsions, vomiting, fainting, and paralysis. Mesmer studied her symptoms until he was able to predict when they were about to recur. Then he made her swallow a preparation containing iron and attached three magnets to her body, one on her stomach and two on her legs. She soon reported that she felt streams of a mysterious fluid flowing through her body. The sensation was not pleasant and relaxing. Rather she experienced something like violent convulsions, an effect that Mesmer named the *crisis*. The treatment continued for several hours after which the crisis subsided and she reported that her symptoms were much improved.

The next year Mesmer took a blind patient into his home in an attempt to restore her sight. Maria-Theresia Paradis, who was 18-years-old, had been blind since the age of three. The daughter of a wealthy civil servant, she had received the best medical care available but it had not helped her blindness. To the contrary, some of the treatments in use at the time undoubtedly made her problem worse including more than 3000 electrical shocks delivered directly to her eyes.[5] After a number of sessions with Mesmer, in which he did not use magnets but only his hands and a wand,[6] she reported that she could see, but a medical commission that examined her noted that she claimed to see only when Mesmer was present. A terrible conflict broke out between Mesmer and the girl's parents that culminated in the father forcing his way into Mesmer's house with his sword drawn and demanding the return of his daughter. Depressed by the incident, Mesmer left Vienna and went to Paris. In Paris Mesmer became successful and celebrated. Many of his patients were fashionable and wealthy, but he also treated men and women of modest means, though not in the same room as the aristocratic patients. His cures were dramatic. The patients sat around a large enclosed tub, called the *baquet*, in which there were jars of water that Mesmer had previously "magnetized." Each patient held a metal rod that projected down into the tub. At the appointed time Mesmer, accompanied by music and dressed in purple robes, would enter the room and make passes with his hands around the body of each patient. He believed that he no longer needed iron magnets, because he believed that he could transmit magnetism from his own body to the patients through his hands. The results were remarkable. His patients would swoon, cry out, and slump into a faint. An assistant helped the patients to another room where they could recline and recover. Many reported later that they were cured.

The controversy that Mesmer tried to escape in Vienna, however, followed him to Paris. Other physicians ridiculed his magnetic cures and in 1784 convinced the king of France to establish a commission to investigate Mesmer. The commission was headed by Benjamin Franklin, one of the foremost scientists of the day, who was serving in France as the first United States ambassador. Franklin and the other commissioners conducted a thorough investigation the crux of which was a test that took place in Franklin's garden in a Paris suburb. One of Mesmer's disciples, Charles D'Eslon, was invited to "magnetize" a tree that stood in the garden. A boy, who had previously been susceptible to Mesmer's methods, was then sent into the garden. The commissioners reasoned that, if Mesmer's theory was correct, the boy would be attracted to the tree. The boy did respond but to the wrong tree and consequently the commissioners declared that Mesmer's cures were simply the result of suggestion. This simple test debunked the theory of animal magnetism. Mesmer was denounced as a charlatan, left Paris, and finished his life along the shores of Lake Constance near where he was born.

A secret appendix to the Royal Commission's report was especially damaging. Mesmer, and all his followers who practiced animal magnetism, were men.

Their subjects were largely, but not exclusively, women. The Commission suggested that animal magnetism fostered erotic attractions between female subjects and their male magnetizers. Although Mesmer usually healed by passing his hands over the body of a subject without touching it, there were times when he and his followers "sat with the patient's knees enclosed between their own and ran their fingers all over the patient's body...It was widely believed that mesmerizing was a sort of sexual magic."[7] Popular cartoons and ribald songs characterized Mesmer as a charlatan and seducer. This image persisted throughout the 19th century and 100 years later achieved iconic status in du Maurier's fictional character Svengali.

Hypnosis is not sleep

Mesmer believed that what we now call hypnosis was a physical force, a kind of magnetism that he exuded from his body. A related belief, that hypnosis is a mental state related to sleep is similarly wrong but still widely held. It derives from one of Mesmer's aristocratic disciples, a wealthy nobleman named the Marquis de Puységur. Like Mesmer, Puységur thought that the cures he obtained involved "animal magnetism," but the effects that he observed were very different from Mesmer's. One of his first patients was a young peasant named Victor Race who suffered from a respiratory disease.

When Puységur "magnetized" him, Race did not exhibit a convulsive crisis like Mesmer's subjects, perhaps because it would have been unseemly for him to do so in the presence of nobility. Rather, he fell into a kind of sleep in which he seemed to be more awake than in his normal state. Puységur was struck by the resemblance of this state to sleep-walking or somnambulism. He concluded that the two states were essentially the same but that they differed in the manner in which they were produced and in the matter of rapport.[8] He referred to the waking component of this new state as the *perfect crisis* and called its resemblance to sleep *artificial somnambulism*. In the mid-19th century a British physician named James Braid proposed that a better name for artificial somnambulism was *hypnosis*, and that term has stuck to the present day.

Puységur mesmerized Race on a number of occasions and even took him to Paris where he used him in demonstrations. On one occasion Race confided to Puységur that he was worried about a quarrel that he had had with his sister. It was not something that he would have talked about in his normal state, but he did discuss it when mesmerized. In the "magnetic" state Puységur suggested that he look after his own interests and find a satisfactory resolution of the dispute, which Race subsequently did. This obscure event, that took place 200 years ago, is apparently the first recorded instance of anyone undergoing what we would today call psychotherapy.

Hypnosis was not readily adopted by the medical community. There were, and still are, too many bizarre and unsupported claims regarding it. One of these is that hypnosis is a form of supernatural consciousness through which one can contact the dead, particularly one's own previous lives. There is no scientific support for such claims. In other cases novelists wrote fictional accounts of hypnosis that were totally fallacious. In his story *The Facts in the Case of M. Valdemar*, for example, Edgar Allan Poe wrote about a mesmerist who put a man into a suspended hypnotic state at the moment of death. He remained that way until an attempt was made to awaken him at which time "his whole frame at once...absolutely rotted away beneath my hands. Upon the bed...there lay a nearly liquid mass of loathsome – of detestable putridity."[9] The account is pure fiction. Such a thing never happened and could not happen. For almost two centuries hypnosis has also been used as entertainment at fairs, in theatres, and at parties. Such performances have rarely edified the public or enhanced the image of hypnosis. In one shocking case, for example, a hypnotist in Breslau, Germany attempted to demonstrate the pain reducing powers of hypnosis by cutting his young female assistant with a sharp razor and firing darts at her upper body through an air rifle. Police stopped the demonstration when they observed that the woman was bleeding severely. She later admitted that she always felt pain when cut and that it was especially severe when she was hit by the darts.[10]

Throughout all of this strange history the notion persisted that hypnosis requires a state of sleep or trance but the evidence does not support this view. Consider the following example. One of the most impressive uses of hypnosis is to reduce, and in some cases obliterate, pain. Some individuals have even undergone surgical operations without any other anesthesia than hypnotic suggestion. One of the first surgeons to use suggestion in this way was a Scottish physician named James Esdaile who experimented with mesmerism, as it was then called, at his hospital in Calcutta, India in the early 19th century where he performed several hundred operations. His surgeries included such procedures as draining abscesses and setting bones, but a few were of a more spectacular nature. In one case he removed tumor from a man's scrotum that weighed 80 pounds which the man had used for many years as a writing desk when he sat down.[11] Esdaile believed that mesmerism required the induction of a trance or sleep-like state, often effected by having the patient drink "magnetized" water, but similar results can be achieved with a susceptible subject when there is no mention of hypnosis and no attempt to induce trance.

The author was once asked by a surgeon to work in a hospital with a 13-year-old boy who had been badly burned on one leg. Although he was given medication for pain, the boy was very fearful and became highly agitated, writhing and crying, when the doctors or nurses approached him to tend the burn. With many members of the staff watching the author stood by the boy's bed and began to talk to him. Although he knew who I was I never used the word hypnosis or told him to "look into my eyes," or "go to sleep." Instead I chatted with him for a while and discovered that he liked to think about space travel. I asked him to tell me a story about going into space. Telling the story seemed to help him to relax. After a while, as the story went on, I suggested that he close his eyes so that he could tell the story better and he complied. A little later I said: "In a few moments the doctor may do something to your leg, but that won't bother you. You won't even feel it. You and I are out here in space, whereas your leg is way back on earth." Shortly thereafter the surgeon began to debride the burn, that is, to cut away burned tissue surgically to promote healing. In the past the staff had to hold the screaming boy down during this procedure, but this time he remained calm throughout, and even laughed a bit as he told a joke about the space trip. After it was over the boy was calm, the surgeon was pleased, but one nurse was not impressed. "Humph," she said, "Is that all it is? It's just suggestion," and she was right. Some critics might argue that because the boy knew who I was my very presence, or my suggestion that he close his eyes, induced in him a state of trance. To define trance in such a broad way, however, so that virtually anything may be cited as a criterion for inducing it, makes the definition meaningless.

Many studies have looked for physiological differences between hypnotized and non-hypnotized individuals using measurements of respiration, cardiovascular function, the genitourinary system, metabolism, skin sensitivity, eye movements, and the central nervous system. None has produced a physiological profile that is unique to hypnosis as a special state of consciousness. A comprehensive review of such studies stated: "In reviewing the literature on the somatic effects of hypnosis, we paraphrase William James's comment about the literature on emotion: It would be more rewarding to count and catalog the rocks of New Hampshire than to reread the literature on the somatic effects of hypnosis...Are observed alterations in physiological processes specific to the hypnotic 'trance?' The answer is an unqualified no."[12]

Studies that compare hypnosis to sleep are part of this body of literature. They do not prove that hypnosis is a distinct state of consciousness or a stage of sleep. Rather, they show that hypnosis resembles a relaxed waking state. There are highly valid and reliable ways of measuring the sleep state using electroencephalogram brain wave recordings (EEG). In a comprehensive study, patterns of EEG activity across different regions of the brain were compared between a group of subjects who went to sleep for approximately eight hours in a laboratory and another group, pre-screened for hypnotic ability, who participated in a 30-40 minute session of hypnosis. Brain waves for the hypnosis subjects were recorded when they had reached a certain depth of hypnosis as determined by a hypnotherapist. The results revealed that: "Changes in the spatial structure of distant relationships in the cerebral bioelectric potential field during the transition from wakefulness to light and deep hypnotic states followed patterns entirely different from those observed during natural sleep."[13] Even if a hypnotized person looks and acts as if he or she is in a sleep-like trance, brain wave recordings reveal that that is not the case.

Regression and the supernatural

One of the most intriguing and controversial phenomena of hypnosis is regression to an earlier age. Some believe that a hypnotized individual can be regressed to a time before birth and enter a spiritual world of reincarnation. If true that would place hypnosis outside the realm of scientific examination within psychology, assuming that the supernatural realm is not bound according to the laws of nature. It would also render less plausible the thesis presented here that the power of suggestion is the result of a personality trait that operates in everyday life as effectively as under special circumstances defined as hypnotic. Despite a great deal of hype for reincarnation the evidence for any such effects through hypnosis is ambiguous and negligible. The topic must be dealt with, however, because of the legions of committed trance theorists who believe firmly that they discovered a past life through hypnosis that they could never have accessed in their waking personality.

Given the right suggestions certain individuals can recall a past event so vividly that they seem to be reliving it. In a typical case a hypnotized man may be told that upon the count of five he will find himself back again at his fifth birthday and enjoy it just as he did once before. The hypnotist counts to five and then asks the man to describe where he is and what he is doing. If the regression is effective the man may begin to speak in a childlike voice talking about his party, his playmates that are there, and the presents he got. Given a pencil and asked to write his name he may grab it clumsily and begin to print in the large block letters typical of children. The experience can be so convincing that an observer might believe it to be completely truthful. The fact is, however, that such memories cannot be relied upon. An adult relative who was there and remembers the day may find errors and inconsistencies in the account. The man, for example, might insist that his birthday cake was chocolate, whereas his mother may recall that it was angel food and that he did not have a chocolate cake until he was six years-old. This is very important because the truthfulness, or veridicality, of memories recalled in this way has been a crucial point in certain court cases of alleged childhood sexual abuse.

Hypnotic age regression has been used in psychotherapy for more than one hundred years. In 1956, however, the use of regression took a radically different turn. Morey Bernstein, a businessman and amateur hypnotist from Pueblo, Colorado, reported that he had regressed a woman whom he called Ruth Simmons not simply to an earlier age, but before birth to a previous life in which she claimed that her name was Bridey Murphy.[14] Many people viewed the report as scientific evidence for a

23

soul that survives death and for a spirit world that can be accessed through hypnosis.

Bernstein's experiments became the foundation for a widely sought approach to therapy in which troubled individuals seek to find the causes for their problems in previous lives. One practitioner, Dick Sutphen, says that he has regressed more than 150,000 people in group sessions and thousands individually.[15] Troubled individuals, he says, often don't find the source of their anxiety, depression or phobias by consulting traditional psychologists or psychiatrists, but using regressive hypnosis, he says, he always finds the cause. Many psychologists and psychiatrists practice regression therapy. Web based directories list scores of practitioners in more than 20 American states and many countries. It has been embraced by Hollywood stars. Actor Glenn Ford discovered through regression that he was once a Christian martyr who was eaten by a lion, and singer Loretta Lynn was a Cherokee princess. One of the best known proponents is actress Shirley MacLaine who claims to have been beheaded in a previous life by King Louis XV of France. MacLaine says that learning of her beheading helped to cure her of stage fright.

The alleged ability of a deceased individual's soul to be reborn into another person is called reincarnation. It is interesting to trace where Bernstein got the idea for regressing Simmons to an earlier existence. Reincarnation was foreign to the Judeo-Christian tradition that dominated America in the 1950s and which is still professed by the majority of Americans today. Reincarnation is a tenet, however, of both Buddhism and Hinduism. Neither had a large number of American adherents then, but cultural changes were taking place which, barely a decade later, would place Bernstein's work at the center of the revival of mysticism that became the Hippie movement of the 1960s.

Another precursor to Bernstein's work was spiritual healing. An acquaintance called his attention to the work of Edgar Cayce, sometimes called the Sleeping Prophet of Virginia Beach, who allegedly diagnosed illnesses by clairvoyance. During the years 1901-1944 Cayce gave readings on various health problems in some 9000 recorded cases. One woman was described to him, for example, as suffering from incurable scleroderma, an autoimmune disorder that can affect the skin, with "inroads of a tubercle." Cayce suggested sponging the area off with a saturated solution of bicarbonate of soda (baking soda) followed by hot castor oil packs. The woman's skin condition allegedly cleared up.[16]

It was through reading about Cayce that Bernstein became interested in reincarnation. He was particularly impressed by the book *Many Mansions* by Gina Cerminara which described Cayce's studies of reincarnation including the use of hypnosis. Cayce believed that we all go through reincarnation not to repeat destructive life patterns, but until we reach a state of oneness with God. Dying as he did during World War II, his message was particularly poignant. Cerminara said of it: "If indeed the soul of man has many mansions, now, of all times, is the time we need to know the truth..." With this background Bernstein was ready to send Ruth Simmons, whose real name was later revealed to be Virginia Tighe, back to a previous life. The first session took place at Bernstein's home late one Saturday night in November, 1952. Bernstein had worked with Tighe twice before and had regressed her to the age of one. This time he hypnotized her and asked her to go "back...back...back, way back into time and space." He suggested that she might remember faraway lands and distant places and that eventually she would talk to him about a particular scene that she was experiencing. He asked what she was seeing and she said that she had scratched the paint off her metal bed. He asked her name, and she said that it was "Friday Murphy," which Bernstein later corrected to Bridey Murphy, and that she lived in the 1800s in Cork, Ireland.

Over a period of months Bernstein regressed Tighe five more times. Their final session took place on October, 1953. Bernstein transcribed the tape recordings that he made of the sessions and published them as *The Search for Bridey Murphy.* The book became an instant best seller, and Bridey Murphy became a cultural phenomenon. People held "come as you *were* parties." A Houston bar invented a "reincarnation cocktail." Four popular song records came out based on the story, and 30,000 LP recordings of the first taped Bridey Murphy hypnosis session were sold. A film with the same title as the book appeared in 1956 starring Teresa Wright and Louis Hayward. Bernstein's book continues to sell well today.

Bernstein cites several points to support his claim that Virginia Tighe experienced an earlier life through hypnosis. One was that other witnesses to the sessions were convinced that Tighe was not shamming, that is, that she believed in the truthfulness of her experience. A second was that she spoke with a pronounced Irish brogue that Bernstein found convincing. A third was her ability to dance a jig that she had talked about as Bridey after she was awakened from hypnosis. A fourth was Bernstein's belief that her account was too drab and unromantic to have come from some story that she might have read. Bernstein further states that he was able to confirm that there were in Belfast at the time grocers named Carrigan and Farr from whom Bridey claimed to have shopped. On the other hand Bernstein could not locate any book called *The Green Bay* nor could he locate any church in Belfast named St. Theresa's, both of which she had mentioned

None of these points is solid evidence for reincarnation. As noted earlier individuals who are experiencing a hypnotic regression are often convincing, although their accounts may later be proved false. The ability to dance a jig or speak with a brogue doesn't amount to much either. Most Americans of Tighe's day had seen and heard such things in the movies or had come into contact with Irish-American immigrants. On the other hand her apparent knowledge of certain facts about Belfast is intriguing.

Shortly after *The Search for Bridey Murphy* was published, William Barker, a reporter for the *Denver Post,* spent three weeks in Ireland seeking confirmation of her story. His findings were later published as a supplement to the newspaper. While in Belfast he focused on Bridey's allegation that her husband Brian wrote articles on the law for the *News-Letter.* He attempted to read the paper for the years 1843-1864 but gave up after it took 45 minutes just to go through one month's issues. He later concluded that he doubted that anyone had ever made a thorough check of this source nor he did think anyone ever would. Barker's report is largely devoted to refuting various criticisms of Bridey's account. They included whether or not she could have had a metal bed at the time she said she did; whether or not Irishmen could have practiced law during the years of British domination; whether or not the wooden house that she described in Cork could have existed in a land where wood is scarce; whether the meals that Bridey said she cooked and enjoyed were appropriate to the time and circumstances; and whether her own wake, which she describes from some vantage point after her death, could have occurred as she describes it. In the end Barker's researches were inconclusive. In an appendix to Bernstein's book he says that he could find "neither for nor against Bridey."[17]

A Chicago tabloid was less equivocal. The *Chicago American* published an alleged exposé, based on interviews with people who claimed to have known Virginia Tighe, which said the Bridey Murphy personality was simply a composite of recollections from Tighe's childhood in the 1930s. This finding became the final word for skeptics, and it is widely quoted today. The website *The Skeptic's Dictionary*, for example, says: "No records were found that matched Tighe's claims for Bridey's birth, upbringing, marriage, or death...One newspaper, however, the *Chicago American,* found a Bridie Murphy Corkell in Wisconsin in the 20th century. She lived in the house across the street from where Virginia Tighe grew up. What Virginia reported while hypnotized were not memories of a previous life but memories from her early childhood."[18]

William Barker of the *Denver Post* examined the claims made in the *Chicago American* and which later appeared in *Life* magazine. He found that a clergyman, the Rev. Wally White, helped to prepare the exposé on the grounds that Tighe had attended Sunday School at his church, but Tighe denied ever seeing White until he came to her door in 1956 and said he wanted to pray for her. As for Bridie Murphy Corkell, Tighe denied ever talking to her, and Barker uncovered that Corkell's son John was editor of the Sunday *American* newspaper in which the claims against Bridey first ran.[19]

In addition to skeptics who questioned the Bridey story because it invoked the supernatural, and others who castigated it because their religious beliefs excluded reincarnation, psychiatrists and psychologists objected to it for scientific and professional reasons. Shortly after *The Search for Bridey Murphy* appeared in print six psychiatrists and psychologists, who were well-known hypnosis practitioners, published a rejoinder.[20] It appears to be hurriedly put together. One chapter of the book concerns "miraculous healing and ostensibly supernatural phenomena" and has nothing directly to do with Bridey Murphy. The other chapters review the nature and phenomena of hypnosis, discuss Bridey's claims as fantasies or multiple personalities induced by suggestion, and dismiss Bernstein as an amateur and quack who innocently believed that he made a great discovery.

In support of these views one contributor tells the story of a man who, while under hypnosis, began to speak Oscan, a long dead language that was spoken in third century Italy. He had never studied Oscan or even Latin to which it was related. One can imagine how this event might have evolved into an elaborate story of an earlier life almost two thousand years before. It had, however, a much simpler explanation. The man, who was a student, had been daydreaming in the university library one day when his eyes fell on an open textbook where he read the Oscan *Curse of Vibia*. He apparently memorized the curse without remembering that he had done so because Vibia reminded him of the name of his girlfriend.

The contributors to the scientific rejoinder made no attempt to evaluate the evidence for or against the Bridey Murphy story. They simply rejected it out of hand as a "hypnotizzy" of interest by the public created by Morey Bernstein's revival of "the old mystical concept of reincarnation." At the time they were writing hypnosis was fighting for a legitimate place among medical and psychological specialties. Over the next 50 years scientists learned a great deal about the nature of hypnosis which is today a respected discipline. Hundreds of research reports have been published about hypnosis that meet the highest standards of scientific rigor. Several hypnosis professional societies exist that require members to have appropriate academic degrees and years of supervised practice. Nevertheless hypnosis is continually dogged by its arcane reputation and hints of impropriety. Even Milton V. Kline, editor of the scientific rejoinder, was disciplined years later for falsifying his academic credentials.[21]

Despite its notoriety and popular appeal, the search for the reincarnated Bridey ended ambiguously. It did not yield strong evidence for reincarnation, nor did it prove that if there is such a thing it can be accessed through hypnosis. Taken as a whole the Bridey story is too heavily weighted with family reminiscences that cannot be substantiated, and that may have been invented by Tighe, to be convincing. There is simply not enough confirmable evidence that anyone named Bridey Murphy ever existed. Nevertheless, based in part on the foundation laid by Bernstein, thousands of people since have looked to past life therapy using hypnosis to solve psychological problems in their current lives.

What accounts for the persistent belief that hypnotized people can contact the dead? Reincarnation is not acknowledged by the majority of the world's religious believers. Judaism, Christianity, and Islam, whose adherents account for more than half of the world's population, reject the possibility of reincarnation across the board and, with a few minor exceptions, have always done so. Nevertheless, reincarnation is a part of the New Age spiritual movement based on astrology that many people in the industrialized world have come to embrace. That movement asserts that the earth is entering a new astrological age, defined by the constellation Aquarius, in which reason and technology will bring about universal love and constructive solutions to human social problems.

Apostles of the coming Age of Aquarius ignore the fact that despite the technological marvels and scientific discoveries of the 20th century it was one of the most violent periods in history. Rigorous thinking, the scientific method, and new machines have not changed human nature, the dark side of which continues to advance. Science has not killed war; it serves it. Some people believe that war is a vestige of a primitive state, and that as humankind progresses war will eventually disappear as tails may have done over the course of human evolution. History does not support such a belief. War has not decreased as a result of human progress it has increased. Stories of alleged reincarnation under hypnosis make fascinating reading. The weight of the evidence, however, does not support the claim that past lives or the realm of the supernatural can be accessed through hypnosis.

3. Hypnotic Susceptibility

So what is hypnosis? Let me begin with an example. One of the most successful hypnotists of the 20th century was psychiatrist Milton Erickson (1901-1980) of Phoenix, Arizona who rejected the passionate sort of exhortation used by many hypnotists in favor in indirect forms of suggestion that subtly changed the subject's orientation to reality, much as advertisements try to do. Successful hypnotists, like successful advertisers, are "those who are skilled at communicating with their patients in the language of metaphor and suggestion."[1] Erickson was famous both for his use of metaphor and his unconventional ways of giving suggestions not to induce a state of sleep, but rather to alter a person's consciousness as might happen during a lecture when one's eyes gaze off into the distance and one's thoughts are elsewhere, in other words to redirect attention.

Erickson's consummate sensitivity to subjects and skill with suggestion are illustrated by the following story that involves what Erickson called the *pantomime* technique.[2] Erickson was asked to attend and then comment upon a hypnotic induction conducted by another therapist. Upon entering the room, which was an ordinary lecture hall, he noticed a blackboard at the back of the speaker's platform and some colored chalk. As he glanced appraisingly at the audience he also noticed two young women, seated toward the back of the room on opposite sides, who seemed to be listening attentively. When asked to comment on the demonstration, Erickson was highly critical of the autocratic way in which the speaker had conducted it, at which point the speaker, somewhat resentful, invited Erickson to demonstrate how he would use a gentle, permissive approach and indirect suggestions.

The first thing Erickson did was to have three chairs placed on the platform and to stress that the center chair was for him. Without explanation, he then took out two handkerchiefs and stepped around to the rear of the desk. With his hands out of view of the audience he placed a piece of yellow chalk in one handkerchief and a piece of red chalk in the other. He put one of the handkerchiefs on the floor to the left of the left-hand chair and the other to the right of the right-hand chair. He then sat down on the middle chair and, passing his right arm across his body, noted that the left-hand chair was for one subject and, pointing with his left arm, that the right-hand chair was for another subject. He then began a lecture on the use of indirect suggestions that was punctuated from time to time by his touching each chair in turn and saying that it was for one of the subjects. As the lecture went on Erickson's eyes roamed around the room, but he only looked directly at two members of the audience, the two women that he initially decided were susceptible subjects. Finally Erickson stood up, walked to the middle aisle and, without looking directly at either, said to the two women: "Now that you are ready – slowly stand up and walk down and take your proper seats." At this point the woman who had been seated on the right side of the room walked forward, crossed over, and sat on the left, whereas the woman who had been on the left side of the room walked forward and sat on the right. He then asked the original speaker to open the handkerchiefs so as to prove that the women had taken the correct seats. Baffled, the speaker opened the handkerchief beside the left chair and found a piece of yellow chalk in it. The woman seated in that chair was wearing a yellow dress. When he opened the other handkerchief it contained a piece of red chalk, and, sure enough, the woman on that side was wearing a red dress. Although Erickson obviously knew in advance how things would turn out, he never addressed the women directly before they came to the front of the room. Rather, he used subtle cues and indirect suggestions to produce what must have been an astonishing demonstration to watch. The entire session was a conversation between Erickson and the two women, although no one else realized that fact at the time. There were many other people in the room who heard exactly the same words but did not leave their seats or in any sense become hypnotized. Erickson's demonstration worked because of his skill in selecting the right subjects: women who seemed to be paying attention and responding to what he was saying. The primary factor at work was not so much Erickson's hypnotic ability, although that was important, but rather the suggestibility of the women.

The importance of an individual's suggestibility in hypnosis, as opposed to some external force, was apparently first recognized by a Portuguese priest Abbé Faria. As early as 1813 Faria contended that success in hypnosis depended less on the hypnotist as on the subject, and he recognized that certain types of individuals were more susceptible to hypnosis than others. Later in the 19th century his views were incorporated into what became known as the Nancy School of hypnosis theory which held that virtually everyone could become hypnotized to some degree as opposed to a rival view that held that only victims of a certain psychological disorder (hysteria) could be hypnotized. The leader of the Nancy School was Hippolyte Bernheim, a distinguished physician and professor of internal medicine who argued that hypnotic cures and other effects were not the result of a special state of consciousness but rather the product of suggestion. According to Bernheim: "One could have discovered these phenomena directly in the waking state, without passing through the unnecessary intermediary of induced sleep; and then the word hypnotism would not have been invented. The idea of a special induced magnetic or hypnotic state provoked by special manoeuvres would not have been attached to these phenomena. Suggestion has been born of the old hypnotism, as chemistry was born of alchemy."[3]

In the 20th century these ideas led to attempts to measure individual differences in hypnotic susceptibility by means of tests which define hypnosis as various phenomena that may occur as the result of suggestion. They include the apparent ability to relive a day from the past (age regression), a reduction in perceived pain (hypnotic analgesia), amnesia for events that occurred during the session, muscular rigidities, hallucinations, dreams, and other effects. These phenomena form the basis of contemporary tests of susceptibility to hypnosis. In 1959 E. R. Hilgard and his collaborator André Weitzenhoffer published *The Stanford Hypnotic Susceptibility Scale (SHSS: Form A)*[4] which became the standard laboratory test for measuring hypnotizability for a generation. M. T. Orne adapted the *SHSS: Form A* for group use and called it the *Harvard Group Scale*. Both contained what Hilgard referred to as a "work sample" of hypnotic suggestions culled from more than 150 years of hypnosis practice and research by previous investigators. Form A included suggestions to feel oneself falling backwards, to feel one's eyes getting heavy and closing, to experience a hallucination of a fly buzzing around the room, to have amnesia for the events that took place during the session, to respond to a suggestion to get up and change chairs upon a cue after hypnosis, and various catalepsies such as the inability to bend one's arm. More advanced scales included suggested dreams, visual hallucinations, auditory hallucinations, and suggestions to go back in time and relive a particular day such as a birthday. These phenomena and others such as analgesia and anesthesia were explored by Mesmer and others within the first 25 years or so of the study of hypnosis and they define what is meant by the term hypnosis.

There are a number of such tests but the idea is the same. The person giving the test provides the subject with some time to focus his or her thoughts and then asks the subject to experience one or more of the phenomena. Scores may be based on a pass-fail basis or on the degree to which the subject reports that he or she felt the suggestion work. A large body of literature shows that scores on such tests are relatively stable, or as psychologists would say, reliable. That is, individuals who take the tests more than once tend to get about the same score regardless of how hard they try to experience the suggestions, how much experience they have had with them, or who is administering the test. In fact there is evidence from twin studies that susceptibility to hypnosis is, in part, an inherited trait[5] and that so-called "hypnotic" phenomena may occur in susceptible individuals in non-hypnotic settings.

Consider the following example. One of the most fascinating phenomena associated with hypnosis is the experience of hallucinations, that is, the perception of sensory experiences in the absence of any physical stimulus. A fairly easy hallucination to experience, often used by stage hypnotists, is to suggest that the subject tastes a piece of lemon or onion in the mouth. Hallucinations can also be visual, and when they occur as a result of suggestion they are quite fascinating. One can suggest to an appropriately suggestible person, for example, that he or she will see three little boxes on a table. In fact the experimenter has placed two boxes on the table let us say, a red one and a blue one, while the subject's eyes were closed. If the suggestion is successful the person will report seeing three boxes with eyes open and describe them perhaps as red, white, and blue. One can then say: "I will now snap my fingers and when I do one box will disappear." It does to the astonishment of the subject who is likely to say: "How did you do that?"

The fact is, however, that certain individuals can experience vivid, hallucinatory images in everyday life whether or not there is any mention of hypnosis. Psychologists call such people eidetic imagers. They are not easy to identify, but various researchers have studied them as far back as the Czech anatomist Jan Purkinje in 1819. In one 1964 study eidetic imagery, defined as a visual image that persisted after visual stimulation in accurate detail, properly colored, and capable of being scanned, was measured in the entire population of an elementary school in New Haven, Connecticut.[6] The researchers found that about eight percent of the children were capable of retaining vivid images for as long as four minutes. The authors did not test the children for hypnotic responsiveness but the percentage of imagers was about the same as the percentage of the population capable of visual hallucinations in hypnosis. In a test of visual hypnotic hallucinations, for example, subjects were asked to see a nonexistent light at one end of an oblong box which actually had a small light bulb glowing at the other end. Approximately 11% of the subjects, who were preselected for exhibiting susceptibility to suggestions, said that they saw the imaginary light. In a book about Evangelical Christians called *Vineyarders*, T. M. Luhrmann discusses visual and auditory experiences reported by church members such as hearing God's voice.[7] Luhrmann avoids calling such experiences hallucinations, preferring instead the term "sensory overrides," but she asserts that between 10 and 15 per cent of the general population has had such experiences. Hypnotic hallucinations, eidetic imagery tested in a school setting, and religious visions may not be identical, but the numbers reported by those who have studied them suggest that approximately 10% of the population, give or take, is capable of experiencing hallucinatory imagery either within or outside the context of hypnosis.

The pervasiveness of hypnotic susceptibility

The question is, then, what proportion of the population is hypnotizable? If the proportion is small then there is less chance that hypnosis can be used as a political or social force than if the percentage is large. In 2010 the popular British stage hypnotist Chris Hughes proposed to demonstrate that he could hypnotize a good part of the world on "World Hypnotism Day" (January 4th) by inducing millions of men and women via Facebook to close their eyes upon the suggestion to do so and to feel their hands tightly held together.[8] There is no way to know how successful Hughes was, but the suggestions that he gave were harmless and not difficult to experience. Very likely a large percentage of those who tried to experience them did. In fact if you close your eyes, hold your hands out in front of you right now, and imagine that you have strong magnets on your palms that are pulling your hands together, you should be able to feel some attraction without being "hypnotized."

Throughout the years other hypnotists have tried to estimate how hypnotizable, on the average, large groups of people are by extrapolating from the results of their own cases. Studies that report population averages for hypnotic susceptibility date back more than a century, but they are difficult to summarize because we do not always know what criteria the researchers used to define the presence or degree of hypnosis. One thing is clear. All of the reports include a certain percentage of individuals who were not hypnotizable at all. That is, some individuals did not close their eyes when asked to do so, they did not look relaxed, they did not feel the suggestions work, and so forth. If we can assume that the inability to be hypnotized looks much the same, regardless of the criteria used to define higher levels of hypnosis, then we can get an idea of the pervasiveness of hypnotic susceptibility simply by the method of subtraction.

In his book *Hypnotism: Its History, Practice and Theory,* (1930) the Scottish physician John Milne Bramwell published the results of susceptibility studies going back to the 1880s.[9] They included the following: between 1882 and 1886 French physician Hippolyte Bernheim reported that he attempted hypnosis with 10,000 individuals and succeeded with 80% for a failure rate approximately 20%; between 1887 and 1890 Dutch physicians Fredrik van Eeden and A. W. van Renterghem attempted to hypnotize 1089 persons and failed with five percent; between 1887 and 1890 French physician Ambroise-Auguste Liébeault, attempted to hypnotize 1756 cases and failed with slightly more than three percent. In 1890 Swedish doctor Otto Wetterstrand reported attempting hypnosis with 3209 individuals of which about four percent were failures, and in 1892, the German physician Albert von Schrenck-Notzing published hypnotic susceptibility statistics from observers in 15 different countries which showed that out of a total of 8705 attempts to hypnotize about six percent were failures. Overall, these studies show a failure rate in attempts to hypnotize of about 11%.

In his book *Hypnotic Susceptibility* (1965) E. R. Hilgard cites results from similar studies from the early 20th century and reports an average failure rate of about nine percent.[10] A summary of later studies dating from 1931 to 1958 involving more than 500 college student subjects reports a failure rate of approximately 17%, and results from the standardization tests of Hilgard's own *Stanford Hypnotic Susceptibility Scales: Forms A & B* show that approximately 10% of subjects were not hypnotizable where failure was defined as responding to not more than one suggestion out of 12 on the test.

In sum the results of tests of hypnotizability dating back more than 125 years, and involving thousands of subjects, show that the vast majority of men and women are hypnotizable to some degree and that only a small percentage, approximately 10% to 15% of the population, are not hypnotizable. Therefore, the commonly heard assertion that a person cannot be hypnotized because his or her mind is "too strong," or that only weak minded people can become hypnotized is for the vast majority of people wrong.

Super subjects

The case for the social relevance of hypnosis is still not made. To say that most human beings comply predictably with the requests or orders of others is to state the obvious. Were that not true we would all be wandering around aimlessly. The fact is, however, that response to suggestions among those who are suggestible is not equal. From the very beginning hypnotists have known that only a small proportion of subjects respond to the unusual or difficult suggestions that characterize what the public knows and sometimes fears as hypnosis. It is these individuals who have the capacity to experience hypnotic amnesia, that is, to perform an act and then forget that they performed it until reminded again by the hypnotist. It is these individuals who will perform an act over and over after a hypnosis session has formally ended when cued to do so by the hypnotist.

Years ago the author was engaged in research at Stanford University's Laboratory of Hypnosis Research that required one individual to be hypnotized repeatedly over a series of weeks. I asked a woman to help me who I knew was an excellent subject. With such a person it is often not necessary to go through a lengthy induction of hypnosis every time. A simple code word may be sufficient. To facilitate the process I suggested that the woman enter hypnosis whenever I said the word "kumquat." I knew that a kumquat was a fruit but I had never seen one and simply thought that it was a catchy word. I had recently moved to the West Coast from the East where kumquats were relatively rare. Our procedure worked beautifully. Each day of testing the woman would sit down, I would say "kumquat," and she would slump into a highly relaxed state of heightened suggestibility during which she could experience visual hallucinations of the sort required in our

41

research. One day, however, she and a friend went to nearby San Francisco where there is a large shopping district of Asian markets. According to the woman's friend as they passed one market that featured a display of kumquats she went in and stood, transfixed, in front of the display. Her friend literally had to drag her out of the shop. Neither understood what had happened, nor did they connect it with our testing until we had a chance to talk about it. We later, of course, changed the code word. The woman was not told to buy kumquats or even to like them. Nevertheless, the word produced a profound effect in her even though she was at a distance both in time and space from her hypnotist. It is these subjects who are the stuff out of which movies like the *Manchurian Candidate* are made.

Various experts have estimated the percentage of individuals capable of such profound effects. George Estabrooks gave the proportion as one in five (20%).[11] In a summary of six studies performed between 1931 and 1958, E. R. Hilgard (1965) reported a range of three to 29% with an average of 13%. The discrepancies result from different criteria used to define hyper-suggestibility. For the *Stanford Hypnotic Susceptibility Scale: Form A*, perhaps historically the most widely used test, Hilgard reported that 11% of subjects fell into the category he called "very high," defined by a score of 11 or 12, out of 12, on the test. During my years there the Stanford laboratory often used a criterion of nine or greater on the test to define high susceptibility, a criterion that would include approximately 23% of those tested. Overall, Estabrooks estimate that about one person in five is capable of the most profound effects of suggestion seems reasonable.

The significance of all this is that whereas most individuals are pushed and pulled by the suggestions we all encounter in life, about one fifth of the population may be affected far more deeply. In the marketplace of commercial messages where competition is fierce the social danger may be primarily that some folks stuff their closets with more goods than others. In the political realm the danger seems greater. During American elections vast sums are given to candidates and to the political action committees that favor them which, in the final analysis, are nothing more than bribes. What candidate will deny that a donation of hundreds of thousands or millions of dollars to a campaign does not at least warrant the slightest piquing of attention?[12] We are on dangerous ground. The tsunami of dollars that surge past the majority of voters may force a small minority of people into eddies of fanaticism, hatred and violence.

Media seduction of children

Suggestibility measured in the context of hypnosis not only varies between individuals but also varies with age. It is difficult to test very young children, who may not understand what they are being asked to do, but once they have reached school age suggestibility scores increase to a peak between the ages of seven and 14 before declining to adult levels at around age 15. The first study of hypnotic susceptibility in childhood was performed by A. A. Liébeault more than 125 years ago. It was based on susceptibility tests given to more than 700 children and adults. More than 50% of children between ages 7 and fourteen scored highly on tests of susceptibility that he administered, whereas in adults the percentage who scored highly was approximately 20% corresponding to the figure cited earlier. In his book *Hypnotic Susceptibility*,[13] E. R. Hilgard cites similar results from three other published studies that involved more than 1300 children. Given that studies have shown a correlation between hypnotic susceptibility and compliance with suggestions in everyday life, the relatively high susceptibility of children raises issues in view of the intense level of advertising aimed at children and young teens.

Advertising aimed at children often ties products to toys, movies, television programs, or cartoon characters that children favor. In his book *Fast Food Nation*,[14] for example, Eric Schlosser details how the McDonald's Corporation for decades patterned its marketing to that of the Walt Disney Company. In fact Ray Kroc, who bought out the McDonald brothers and founded the McDonald's empire, and Walt Disney were old friends. They were about the same age, were both from Illinois, and had served together in the same World War I ambulance corps. McDonald's success has set the standard for other advertisers to children.

The economic stakes are very high. According to one study US adolescents spend as much as $140 billion a year. Children under 12-years-of-age may spend another $25 billion and influence another $200 billion of spending by adults. In response US advertisers allocate more than $1 billion on media advertising to children, mostly on television; over $4.5 billion on youth-targeted promotions such as premiums, sampling, coupons, contests, and sweepstakes; and about $2 billion on youth-targeted public relations, such as broadcast and print publicity, event marketing, and school relations. In addition, roughly

$3 billion is spent on packaging especially designed for children.[15]

A special case of rhetoric

The preceding sections have attempted to present the case that there is such a thing as hypnosis, that most people can experience it, that it is not the result of the power of the hypnotist, and that it does not require a state of sleep or trance. So what is it? I would propose that hypnosis is nothing more than a special case of rhetoric, the name we give to the effective use of language to persuade, and that its power depends upon the suggestibility of the listener.

The use of rhetoric can probably be traced through the market stalls and caravans of the ancient world to the earliest human communities, but the formal study of persuasion began in ancient Greece about 400 BC in the movement known as sophism. The sophists were skeptics who doubted the possibility of attaining true knowledge of anything. They emphasized the practical application of rhetoric in civic and political life. Some claimed that they could teach both a thing and its opposite, simultaneously arguing both thesis and antithesis. One of the founders of sophism was Gorgias a Sicilian philosopher, orator, and rhetorician who settled in Athens where over his long life of 108 years he made large sums of money from his lecturing. Gorgias loved paradoxes and went to great length to make absurd arguments appear strong. He was not, however, just an entertainer or oratorical trickster. He believed that we can never directly know what truly exists but only know existence through the language that we use to describe it. In his essay *On Nature,* Gorgias stated his main ideas which were that: (1) Nothing exists; (2) If

45

anything does exist it is unknowable; and (3) If anything can be known it is incommunicable. The point that Gorgias was making is that people cannot truly understand one another because we perceive the world differently. Since different people have different ideas about the same things there can be no ultimate reality. Gorgias was, in other words, a relativist or phenomenologist who held the view that there is no general truth but only what appears to be true for a single individual. Protagoras, another great sophist, said it this way: "Man is the measure of all things: of things which are, that they are, and of things which are not, that they are not." Other philosophers accused the sophists of unsound reasoning and of using false arguments to win their point. Plato regarded them as dishonest, and the term sophistry still connotes fallacious reasoning, but the sophists understood the power of persuasion. Gorgias argued that persuasive words had power equivalent to that of the gods. In the *Enconium,* his defense of Helen of Troy against the claim that she caused the Trojan War, Gorgias compares the effect of speech on the soul to the bodily effect of drugs. He says: "Just as different drugs draw forth different humors from the body – some putting a stop to disease, others to life – so too with words: some cause pain, others joy, some strike fear, some stir the audience to boldness, some benumb and bewitch the soul with evil persuasion."[16] He believed that his "magical incantations" could control powerful emotions and heal the psyche. He paid particular attention to the sounds of words with which, according to one historian, he delivered in a florid, rhyming style that seemed to hypnotize his audiences.[17]

Despite the alleged preeminence of reason, especially scientific reasoning, in the current world it is probably true today, as throughout the past 2500 years, that the opinions and beliefs of most people most of the time are shaped more by rhetoric than by logic. In the long saga of human history periods of rationality stand like tufts of firm ground in a vast swamp of drivel. That this is the case in human affairs speaks to the overwhelming power of persuasion to trump pure reason.

Human beings are primed by nature to respond to suggestions given by the right person in the right context. The right context is one in which the suggestions resonate with a human need such as to feel less pain. The right person is one who projects both the authority and the confidence that he or she can cause the desired change. Sometimes the context in which suggestions are given is trivial, as when hypnosis is demonstrated in a college fraternity house. The subjects' motives for responding range from simple fakery to a desire to show off. In other cases suggestions pierce the human soul and touch the deepest desires of a people. That happened in Nazi Germany and in a very different way it happens today when the media use suggestions to stimulate desire for material goods.

4. Hitler and the Rise of Nazism

It is no accident that in 1920, at the dawn of radio, an obscure German war veteran gave his first major speech in a Munich beer hall that ultimately catapulted him to world infamy. In it he presented a 25-point plan for the restoration of Germany which had been impoverished by the peace treaty that ended World War I. His name was Adolf Hitler and the plan became the foundation of the Nazi Party. Although broadcast radio did not begin in Germany until 1923, radio quickly became the major vehicle by which Hitler was propelled into power. American historian William Shirer wrote: "radio became by far the regime's most effective means of propaganda, doing more than any other single instrument of communication to shape the German people to Hitler's ends."[1] Hitler and radio grew up together and he used it extensively to shape and control public opinion but the 1934 Nazi Party Congress in Nuremberg also revealed his mastery of film. He served as unofficial producer of Leni Riefenstahl's powerful documentary of the Congress titled *Triumph of the Will,* which was characterized by speeches, images of Hitler as a religious figure, and massed Nazi troops. It is still regarded by critics as one of the greatest films ever made.[2]

The combination of Adolf Hitler and the mass media was cataclysmic. In the long and bloody history of humanity many tyrants and mass murderers have occupied center stage for a time and passed on. Even among the worst Hitler stands out. Consider the following:

(1) in 1933 approximately nine million Jews lived in the European countries later occupied by the Nazis. By the end of the war six million of them were dead, annihilated in Nazi death camps. (2) One-and-a-half million children were murdered by the Nazis during World War II including 1.2 million Jewish children, tens of thousands of Gypsy children, and thousands of disabled children. (3)Total deaths in World War II are estimated to be between 68 and 72 million making it the deadliest war ever, including 40-52 million civilians and five million prisoners of war.

How was it that Germany, which before World War I was a religious and cultivated nation with a rich tradition of science, technology, and music could become so deeply infected with the hatred that produced Auschwitz, Treblinka, Dachau, and Buchenwald? What igniting of elements rocketed Hitler from obscurity to global infamy in less than 25 years? Some blame the catastrophe squarely on Hitler himself and his ability to sway the masses. Hitler was charismatic. Women fell in love with him. Men gave their lives for him. One woman who found him attractive was Martha Dodd, daughter of the United States Ambassador to Berlin, who met Hitler on several occasions. She said of him that his eyes: "were startling and unforgettable – they seemed pale blue in color, were intense, unwavering, hypnotic."[3]

Hitler was a master orator whose words had great effect, but was he a Svengali or was he simply the means by which the German people released decades of pent-up hatred and violence? Nothing about his early life suggests any unusual powers. Hitler was born in the city of Brunau am Inn in upper Austria in 1889, the son of a customs official. In 1894 the family moved to Linz about 55 miles to the east, and Hitler grew up in and around that city. At age

16 Hitler quit school and moved to Vienna to study art where he was twice rejected by the Academy of Fine Arts. He lived the Bohemian life of an unsuccessful painter there until he was drafted into the army in World War I. He served as a runner with a Bavarian reserve regiment on the Western Front, was wounded and decorated twice for bravery with the Iron Cross. During the war Hitler became a great admirer of Germany, Austria's ally, and he was devastated when Germany surrendered to the Allies in November, 1918.

Hitler joined the small German Worker's Party in 1919 which he took over in 1921 and renamed the National Socialist Workers' (NAZI) Party. In 1923 the Nazis under Hitler's leadership joined right-wing Bavarian leaders in an uprising against Germany's Weimar government. They were put down by the police who killed 16 Nazi supporters, and Hitler was arrested and sentenced to nine months in prison. During that time he wrote *Mein Kampf* (My Struggle), a virulently anti-Semitic autobiographical statement of Hitler's political views. By 1932 the Nazi party had become the largest constituent in the German Reichstag (parliament). The next year Hitler became Chancellor, declared the Nazi party to be the only legal party in Germany, and, in 1934 succeeded Paul von Hindenburg as president upon Hindenburg's death.

After 1934 events spiraled rapidly toward the abyss of war. Guessing correctly that Great Britain and France would do nothing to stop him, Hitler's forces reoccupied the Rhineland in 1936, which had been demilitarized by the Treaty of Versailles, and later took over Austria and Czechoslovakia allegedly to give Germany more *lebensraum* (living space). His campaign of military expansion culminated in the invasion of Poland in 1939 which precipitated World War II.

We know that Hitler was aware of hypnosis. He was hypnotized in 1918 after being blinded by a British mustard gas attack that occurred while he was serving with the 16th Bavarian Reserve Infantry Regiment. His blindness was diagnosed as being at least in part hysterical (psychological) and he received psychiatric treatment from Dr. Edmund Forster at Pasewalk Military Hospital in northern Germany.

We also know that Hitler was an accomplished orator who carefully practiced his speeches before a mirror. In the early days of his career, when many of his speeches were delivered in beer halls, Hitler paced his ranting to the intoxication of the crowd for maximum effect until his voice became hypnotic, a tribute in part to the coaching of actor and voice-trainer Paul Devrient. From the beginning Hitler's effect on Germany was called hypnotic, even by his harshest critics. In describing his domination of the German Workers' Party, for example, Sir Winston Churchill said of Hitler that: "By the middle of the following year, (1921) he had ousted the original leaders, and by his passion and genius forced upon the hypnotized company the acceptance of his personal control."[4]

The Treaty of Versailles of 1919 which formally ended the war imposed harsh economic terms on Germany justified by the claim (Article 231) that Germany was to blame for the entire war. It stated: "The Allied and Associated Governments affirm and Germany accepts the responsibility of Germany and her allies to causing all the loss and damage to which the Allied and Associated Governments and their nationals have been subjected as a

MEDIA HYPNOSIS IN ADVERTISING AND POLITICS

consequence of the war imposed upon them by the aggression of Germany and her allies." The total sum due from Germany for war reparations was roughly the equivalent of $400 billion current US Dollars, a sum that many economists deemed to be excessive. The amount was reduced by more than half later that year but it was still too large in the eyes of most Germans because at the terms offered it would have taken Germany 60 years to pay it off. The treaty's demands were impossible to meet, and in fact, Germany's postwar economic recovery was in part financed by loans from the United States. The recovery was cut short in 1923, however, when France, impatient at the pace of reparation payments, invaded the Ruhr Valley, Germany's industrial heartland. Pressure from France added to already high rates of inflation led to a complete breakdown of the German currency. The exchange rate between the dollar and the mark, which at the beginning of the war had been about four or five to one dollar, became one trillion marks to the dollar. A wheelbarrow full of money would not even buy a newspaper.[5] Millions of ordinary Germans saw their life savings wiped out.

In view of the reparations demanded of Germany Hitler's appeal was initially economic, but Germany also felt the sting of having its once great military machine emasculated. In the post-war spirit of disarmament many nations, including Great Britain, reduced their military forces, but France, Germany's primary opponent in the war, was permitted to retain its large army in the belief that its strength would serve as a counterweight to any German rearmament. Germany was allowed only a small army and no air force. Hitler's success in rebuilding Germany's military forces despite the treaty restrictions, and his many public works projects including building the world's first superhighways, gave many Germans hope for the future.

It would be an unwarranted stretch to blame hypnosis for what happened in Germany during the Nazi era if what one means by hypnosis is that the nation was entranced by special words or powers over which it had no ability to resist. What seems true is that the vast majority of Germans, who were suffering in the aftermath of World War I, were swayed enough by Hitler's message to go along with him. If some later regretted their decision it was by then too late. A smaller but significant number, perhaps more affected by his oratory, became fanatical followers who enforced Hitler's program with brutal violence.

Hitler's propaganda chief, Joseph Goebbels, explained Hitler's persuasive power in the language of rhetoric. He wrote that there are two fundamentally different kinds of speakers: those who use reasoning, and those who speak from the heart. Although Goebbels recognized that Hitler sometimes spoke in reasoned arguments, he believed that Hitler's power lay in his appeal to the emotions. "Those who speak from the heart," he said, "speak to the people." Hitler's voice, he said, reached out from the depths of his blood into the depths of the souls of his listeners. He brought to expression the secrets of the human soul. Author Saul Bellow expressed it this way: "Outer forces inject themselves into us, penetrating the very nervous system. When the individual discovers them inside his own head, their appearance seems to him entirely natural, just as Hitler and the population of Germany spoke a common language."[6] As a result, Goebbels believed that such

53

rhetorical geniuses were the drummers of fate. "They begin their work alone in dark and dismal historical epochs and suddenly and unexpectedly find themselves in the spotlight of new developments. They are the speakers that make history."[7]

Was Hitler a hypnotist? Not if you believe the discredited views that hypnosis involves using some special words or force to turn people into zombies. The entire German nation did not walk around in a trance for six years. But if you believe that a nation, or a large part of a nation, can be swayed by a leader who appeals to the emotions and who suggests actions that individuals accept as steps toward a desired goal, even when those actions are grotesque, then the answer is yes, that he was.

One of the authoritative voices on hypnosis of the mid-20th century was Professor George H. Estabrooks of Colgate University, a school with a long tradition of hypnosis theory and research.[8] In his book *Hypnotism* (1957) Estabrooks wrote: "It has always been the writer's contention that Hitler was the greatest hypnotist of his day, and this statement is not just a play upon words. To be sure Hitler may never have read a book on the subject or known the meaning of the word. We can, I think, make out a convincing case that basically Hitler's emotional domination of the crowd – or speaking professionally, his attack – was only the attack of the stage hypnotist one step removed."[9] The step, however, of which Estabrooks speaks, is a big one. Never before had one individual influenced so many people. The invention of mass media in the 20th century made it possible for large populations of men and women to be influenced by suggestions in a manner and to a degree never before seen.

Hitler's power to persuade was by no means universal. What he did was to use his charisma, combined with the use of film, radio, patriotic symbols, and nationalistic themes to develop a cadre a fanatically loyal Nazi followers who then impressed their views on the broader population by persuasion or violence. In his book *Mein Kampf* he stated: "The highest task of the organization, therefore, is to see to it that no kind of internal disagreements among the members of the movement lead to a cleavage and with it to a weakening of the work in the movement; further, that the spirit of determined aggression does not die out, but that it continuously renews and fortifies itself." Only in this way, he believed, could his revolution with its new view of life be taught to all of the German people: "and, if necessary...later forced upon them."[10] That the threat of force underlay Hitler's every move is illustrated in his relationship with his long-time friend and supporter Ernst Röhm. Röhm was a German army officer and Nazi party leader who founded and later commanded the Sturmabteilung (SA), or Storm Battalion, which was the Nazi party militia. The SA was a political army whose role was to protect Nazi Party leaders, battle communists, and terrorize Jews. Röhm, along with Hitler and several others, was arrested following the unsuccessful revolt of 1923, sometimes called the Beer Hall Putsch, and charged with treason. He was discharged from the army but served no prison time. Röhm was an extremely close friend of Hitler's and allegedly the only one who continued to call him Adolf after he came to power rather than "mein Führer." For five years, from 1925-1930 Röhm served as a military advisor in Bolivia, but he returned to Germany at Hitler's invitation to serve as the SA's Chief of Staff which by that time numbered more than one million members.

The SA's traditional role of protecting party officials had in the meantime been given to the Schutzstaffel (SS) commanded by Heinrich Himmler but the SA continued to intimidate anyone they deemed hostile to the Nazi regime including Jews, intellectuals, politicians, and journalists. The SA had a reputation, however, for street violence, heavy drinking, and homosexuality which eventually led to its downfall. Röhm himself wrote about homosexual liaisons in letters which were subsequently published. Despite his apparent anti-communism, Röhm was a socialist who railed against conservatives and capitalists many of whom Hitler had courted to support his growing militarism. Röhm also came into conflict with the German army, the Reichswehr, which he proposed should be merged into the SA. In 1934 Röhm's enemies within the Nazi Party circulated stories that Röhm and the SA were plotting to overthrow Hitler, and on June 30, 1934, in what was known as the "Night of the Long Knives" Hitler had the SA purged and its leaders, including Röhm, killed. The story serves as an allegory of mass persuasion during the Nazi era. Despite the long friendship between Hitler and Röhm, and despite Hitler's vaunted reputation for charm, charisma, and force of personality, when Röhm fell into disfavor Hitler simply had him shot. Much of the power of mass persuasion in Nazi Germany was the result of terror and thuggery not suggestion. There is no way to know if Hitler's truly devoted followers were at the upper end of the suggestibility scale, but it is certainly true, at least initially, that a large percentage of the German population acquiesced with the Nazi message while a smaller number of Nazi fanatics took over the country.

Some assert that Hitler simply ignited a fuse of hatred that was already deeply imbedded in the German soul. In his book *Hitler's Willing Executioners* (1994) Daniel Goldhagen, the son of a former Harvard professor who survived the Holocaust in a Romanian-Jewish ghetto, asserts that Germany was imbued with a particularly virulent and long-standing anti-Semitism aimed at the eradication of Jews which Goldhagen calls "eliminationist anti-Semitism."[11] This view, he believes, was rife in Germany before World War I and grew more virulent in the Weimar Republic even before Hitler came to power. Goldhagen supports his view that ordinary Germans participated in the Holocaust, not just dedicated Nazis, using data from the German Order Police, that is, ordinary uniformed police units; the use of Jews as forced laborers; and Jewish death marches. One might assume that the Nazis used Jews as forced laborers because of a labor shortage caused by so many other Germans serving in the military, but Goldhagen asserts that the true purpose of putting Jews to work was to humiliate and punish them.

Goldhagen's writings have been the object of withering criticism from reviewers who do not deny the horrors of the Holocaust but who believe that it was not a peculiarly German phenomenon. In their book *A Nation on Trial* Norman Finkelstein and Ruth Birn criticize what they believe was poor scholarship on Goldhagen's part in the flawed use and misinterpretation of archival sources. Finkelstein goes so far as to refer to Goldhagen's work as a "crazy thesis." Finkelstein makes the point that what happened in Germany in the 1930s and 1940s could happen again in another country. The seeds of Nazi hatred, in other words, were not in the German soul but in the human soul. He notes that the 21 German leaders indicted at Nuremberg were among the "best and brightest;" lawyers, a professor, a dentist, and an art expert. Finkelstein quotes an American psychiatrist at the trials who concluded that the defendants were not unique or insane but: "could be duplicated in any country in the world today." He concludes by saying that Goldhagen's book, fixating as it does on the pathologically criminal "fails to even grasp, let alone resolve, the central mystery of the Nazi holocaust,"[12] that is, how ordinary people could commit history's greatest crimes. The sad truth is that human beings will commit bestial and despicable acts against others with relatively little instigation. That fact, and an underlying sympathy for Hitler's message, allowed the terrible malignancy to flourish that became the Third Reich.

Following orders

In 1965 Yale University psychologist Stanley Milgram published the first of a series of studies on obedience.[13,14] The basic set-up was this. Research volunteers who responded to a newspaper advertisement were told that they would be participating in a study of the effects of punishment on learning. Two volunteers at a time drew slips of paper from a hat to determine who would be the teacher and who the learner. The selection process, however, was rigged. A true volunteer was assigned to be the teacher, but the learner was actually a confederate of the experimenter. The alleged learner was then conducted to another room where he or she was strapped to a chair that was attached to an electric shock machine. The controls to the machine, which were on the teacher's side of the wall, consisted of a series of switches labeled from "15 volts – slight shock" to "450 volts." The teacher was instructed to present the learner with pairs of words, punishing him or her for wrong answers by delivering electric shocks starting with the lowest voltage and proceeding to the highest. As the teacher pressed each switch a light flashed on and he or she heard an electric buzz. The learner received no actual shocks. The experimenters simply wanted to see how far the so-called teachers would go in administering what they thought were painful punishments. As the shock level went higher and higher the learner at first grunted, then moaned, then screamed to be let out of the experiment. The experimenter, however, asked the teacher to continue to administer shocks, saying that the experiment depended on seeing it through. What would you do? How far would you go in obeying the experimenter's commands?

Before conducting the experiment Milgram asked people what they would do in those circumstances and most said they would stop administering shocks as soon as the learner began to feel pain. Forty psychiatrists whom he surveyed made the same prediction, that the teachers would stop delivering shocks. Milgram discovered, however, that 63% of the teachers in his study, men aged 20 to 50, complied fully right up to the supposed highest voltage.

Critics were quick to assert that the participants knew that no real harm could come to the alleged learners because Yale University was too respectable an institution to allow such a thing. In other words they believed that the teachers were just playing along. To answer this criticism Milgram repeated the study in an industrial building in another city. As before recruits were solicited through a newspaper advertisement and told that the study was a kind of industrial research. No connection was made with any academic institution. Under these circumstances compliance with the experimenter's commands decreased but it was still high.

A chain reaction

Four components combined in the Nazi era that had never before been mixed to produce a national monster. They were a charismatic speaker, a receptive audience, a medium to convey the speaker's message, and a powerful catalyst: susceptibility to suggestion. The first three elements have been well examined. The catalyst, suggestibility, has been studied in other contexts, but its effects in mass persuasion have been barely explored.

As we have seen, tests of hypnotic susceptibility reveal that most people are moderately influenced by suggestions given in the hypnotic context. Perhaps 20% are profoundly affected. Only a small percentage of people don't respond at all. If the results hold true for non-hypnotic contexts as well then, given the deep penetration and ubiquitous presence of advertising in our society, media messages may have the power to stimulate responses in viewers and listeners that range from superficial to truly mesmeric. The stakes are high. The public are easily gulled. Anyone who believes that the modern man or woman is a free, independent agent, able stand unfazed in the face of a media onslaught of information and misinformation has just not been paying attention. If mass persuasion does not work why would advertisers and politicians spend so much money on it?

5. Suggestion and the Consumer Economy

There is an abiding myth in the American psyche that the nation was founded and is sustained by rugged individualists, men and women who would be immune to the kind of influence that Hitler exerted over Germany. Some might say that it traces back to the early European colonists that had to carve their survival out of a wilderness, to the small band of fur traders and explorers who between 1810-1840 became known as Mountain Men, or to the cowboys who in the later 19th century drove large herds to market across hundreds of miles of open range. In fact few Americans were ever cowboys or mountain men, and even the earliest pilgrims lived in settled communities with clearly defined patterns of social relationships and behavior.

Nevertheless the myth persists and a 20th century icon of American individualism might be Howard Roark, the fictional architect in Ayn Rand's 1943 novel *The Fountainhead.* Roark's life is a continual struggle between his artistic and professional integrity and what he perceives to be the forces of tradition and mediocrity. One of his commissions is an important housing project which he insists must be built exactly according to his design. When he discovers that it has been altered without his consent he dynamites it. Put on trial for his act Roark defends himself with a passionate statement of his commitment to egoism and his belief that less creative men and women are parasites. In part he says: "The creator lives for his work. He needs no other men. His

61

primary goal is within himself. The parasite lives second-hand. He needs others. Others become his prime motive. The basic need of the creator is independence. The reasoning mind cannot work under any form of compulsion. It cannot be curbed, sacrificed or subordinated to any consideration whatsoever. It demands total independence in function and in motive. To a creator, all relations with men are secondary."[1]

Rand's portrayal of Roark as an uncompromising and heroic individualist is a product of her admiration for the German philosopher Friedrich Nietzsche (1844-1900), a harsh critic of Christianity who believed that certain individuals whom he called "supermen" possessed a creative "will to power" which distinguished them from ordinary, inferior human beings. At one point, Rand proposed to include quotations from Nietzsche at the beginning of each chapter of the novel.[2] Nietzsche believed that the emergence of supermen was a consequence of evolution. In the prologue to *Thus Spoke Zarathustra* he says: "What is ape to man? A laughing stock or painful embarrassment. And man shall be that to overman (superman): a laughingstock or painful embarrassment. You have made your way from worm to man, and much in you is still worm. Once you were apes, and even now, too, man is more ape than any ape.... The overman is the meaning of the earth. Let your will say: 'the overman *shall be* the meaning of the earth....'" Nietzsche's concept of the superman was later embraced by the Nazis in support of their belief in Aryan superiority.

Even Roark, however, lived among and interacted with other people. It is almost impossible not to. One person who attempted to do so was the fifth century Christian ascetic Simeon Stylites who lived for 37 years on a small platform atop a pole near Aleppo in Syria. After ascending the first of several poles that he used, each higher than the preceding one, he never came down again until he died in the year 459. The hygienic aspects of his existence stagger the imagination. He is said to have "dripped with vermin."[3] Nevertheless, even he attracted crowds of pilgrims and spectators some of whom did communicate with him by ascending to his perch on a ladder. Others received messages that he wrote. His social contacts, however, were very limited. He refused to allow women to come near his pillar, including even his own mother who herself entered into a monastic life of silence in the same area. In a way Simeon was kind of independent generator of thought power, of the sort admired by Rand, sitting by himself in the wilderness, his inspiration presumably coming only from God.

All human beings, even the most isolated and uncommunicative, live in some sort of social milieu. A handful of geniuses, like Einstein or the fictional Roark, may stand above the crowd, but the implementation of even their ideas requires social interaction. Roark did not put up his building himself. Construction requires laborers, skilled craftsmen and craftswomen, engineers and all manner of specialists and finishers. Pretend for a moment that human intellect is like electrical power and compare Simeon's existence, or that of Howard Roark, to the way electricity is generated and distributed. More than 130 million power poles conduct electricity all across the United States. Every year Americans use them to consume more than 600,000 megawatts of electricity generated by more than 1000 of power plants and solar cells of homes and businesses. The electricity from any one source, however, does not go solely to its own customers. The electricity enters a grid which can be shared with other utilities all across the country. Once it enters the grid it is impossible to identify from which plant or home a particular electron came, and if something goes wrong with the grid the effects can be felt hundreds of miles away from where the problem took place.

The writings of countless novelists who have chronicled the human condition across the ages, anthropologists, historians, scientists of all types, the common sense of ordinary men and women, the team-work of the Space Program, and now the internet, all tell us that the power grid is a better metaphor for human intellectual life than the lone pole standing in the wilderness.

Every man, woman and child is constantly being changed and shaped by the other individuals with whom they come into contact. To prove the point, try this simple demonstration. Next time you are on a crowded sidewalk stop and look up. Continue to look up for a minute or so and then look around you. Most likely you will have attracted a small crowd of other people who, like yourself, are looking up. Human beings are highly social, prewired to be aware of and to respond to what others are doing, what Gabriel Tarde called imitation. There are many ways in which this influence takes place. At one level are simple commands that a person of higher power or status gives to a subordinate. They range from benign directives such as when a mother says: "pick up your clothes," to the order "charge," that may send the subordinate to death. Like other social creatures humans observe leadership hierarchies deferring to those in higher positions than ourselves and yielding to their commands.

The common thread that weaves together these various experiences is the human need to comply with what others are doing and saying. Advertisers often strive to make the reader or viewer feel that he or she is part of a group that shares a desire for a particular product. The influence of group conformity on the judgments of an outsider can be very strong as illustrated by one of the classic experiments of social psychology. A prominent social psychologist of the mid-20th century was Solomon Asch, a professor for many years at Swarthmore College and later at Harvard University. In 1955 Asch published an experiment that showed that social pressure can make a person agree with the judgment of others when he or she knows that they are wrong.[4] In the experiment a volunteer participant was asked to join five other people in performing a simple task. The task was to look at a vertical line drawn on a card and to compare it to three others drawn on another card. (See Figure 5.1) What the volunteer did not know was that the other participants were all confederates of the experimenter who had been instructed to give wrong answers to some of the comparisons. In the example shown below it is obvious that line C on the comparison card matches the standard. What would you say, however, if you were asked to do the task and four people ahead of you said that the correct answer was A? In Asch's original experiment and many variations performed by other people since, thousands of college student volunteers have been put in that situation. When they have been asked to make the comparison on their own, without hearing the judgments of others, they have made mistakes in judgment less than one percent of the time. Asch found, however, that in a group setting in which others uniformly gave wrong answers, approximately one-third of the volunteer participants went along with the group on most its judgments and 75% went along with the group at least once. The Asch experiment did not prove that the volunteers actually perceived the lines differently as a result of group pressure, although some of them may have done so. What it showed was that individuals are likely to acquiesce with the opinions of others in a group under certain conditions

Asch and many other experimenters have studied the effects of various situational variables on conformity such as group size and unanimity. If the group contains fewer than three people, if they are not unanimous, or if one or more people in a larger group disagree with the majority, then conformity goes down. If the contention made here, that an individual's susceptibility to hypnotic suggestion is an important determinant of compliance, then suggestibility should also predict how one will perform in Asch's experimental paradigm. That exact result was reported in 1981 by Morris Shames of Concordia University in Montreal.

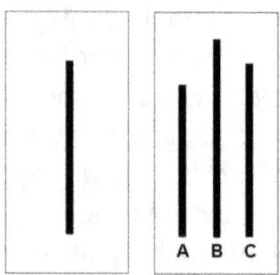

Figure 5.1 Stimuli used in the Asch study of group conformity.

Shames first tested 10 undergraduate participants for hypnotic susceptibility using a test called the *Hypnotic Induction Profile* (HIP). This test was first proposed as a quick way to estimate hypnotic susceptibility by Dr. Herbert Spiegel. It involves simply asking a person to roll his or her eyes upward, the degree of eye roll indicating the degree of hypnotic susceptibility. The test provides a rough estimate of hypnotic susceptibility that correlates only moderately with other measures. Nevertheless, when Shames subsequently asked his volunteers to participate in a line-length estimation task like that devised by Asch he found significant correlations between individuals' hypnotic susceptibility scores and their conformity to the judgments of others on the line estimation task. Shames concluded that "hypnotic susceptibility is a reasonable predictor of conformity, and both appear to be tied to the construct of suggestibility."[5]

Shames study took place in a university laboratory setting which is by its nature removed from everyday life. A stronger comparison would be to test individuals for hypnotic susceptibility using standardized tests that can be administered individually or in a group and then to correlate such scores with a person's response to suggestions in the real world, such as to an advertising campaign or a voter drive, without tipping off the connection between the two tests. Alternatively, one could study a group of people who have already voted or bought a product, but how would one get them to agree to be hypnotized? A study conducted at the author's own laboratory at Muhlenberg College in Pennsylvania overcame these problems by comparing scores on a test of hypnotic susceptibility to archival data, in this case records of giving to a college alumni-annual-giving campaign. The study, performed by Lawrence Greene, compared hypnotic susceptibility scores for 235 college graduates, who had been tested during their student careers, to their records for alumni annual giving over a 10-year period after college. The results showed that those who had made at least one contribution to the college since their graduation were significantly higher in hypnotic susceptibility than those who had made no contribution.[6]

In another study, performed by Lauren Marra, hypnotic susceptibility scores for 458 current and former college students were compared with college yearbook records of their participation in student activities. This was done simply by counting the number of activities, such as teams, sorority, or clubs, which the student listed under his or her photograph in the college yearbook. The results showed that students who were moderately to highly susceptible to hypnosis participated in significantly more student activities than students who were relatively unsusceptible.[7]

Taken together the studies show a striking relationship between hypnosis, as measured by a simple one-hour test, and an individual's responsiveness to suggestions given in a variety of contexts. That single test predicted, on average, which students would participate in campus activities such as teams and clubs during their four-year career and which, years later, would contribute money to the alumni fund. In the future there will undoubtedly be more studies in additional settings, but the significant finding is that there was any relationship at all. It is clear that suggestibility, as measured in the hypnotic context, is relevant far more widely than the previously believed.

Could an individual's susceptibility to hypnotic suggestions affect how he or she responds to the mass media when there is no overt attempt to hypnotize? One study suggests that the answer is yes. Students in communications courses at two colleges were first tested for hypnotic susceptibility by one of the investigators. They were told that the purpose of the demonstration was for them to experience what it was like to be hypnotized. Later in the semester a second investigator who was their professor in the communications course, asked them to watch and rate a documentary videotape. No connection was made between the videotape and the previous hypnosis testing which took place weeks before. The researchers did not predict that the videotape would make the viewers more positive or more negative about the topic. Rather, they wanted to see how much the ratings changed, as a result of viewing the program, regardless of whether they were initially positive or negative. The viewers were asked to complete a simple 10-point rating scale immediately before viewing the tape, immediately afterwards, and again about a week later. On average the viewers changed their initial ratings by approximately 1.5 – 3.0 points immediately following the program. (See Figure 5.2) These differences were not statistically significant as a function of gender, college, or individual differences in hypnotic susceptibility. When the ratings were repeated approximately one week later, however, a striking difference emerged. Students who scored in the upper half on the hypnotic susceptibility test at both institutions tended to retain their changed ratings, whereas the less hypnotizable students, those low in susceptibility, regressed back towards their original positions, and the changes from their previous ratings were statistically significant.[8] A strength of this study is in the fact that it was replicated, that is performed at two different institutions under similar conditions, and the same results were found. These data suggest that the persuasive power of television may be mediated by the same processes of suggestion that are present in hypnosis.

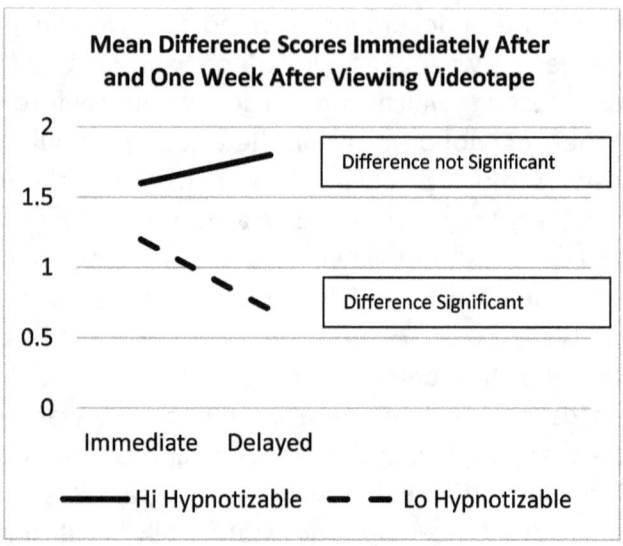

Figure 5.2

Rating scale changes for High and Low susceptible hypnosis subjects immediately after viewing a video program and one week later

Torches of Freedom

No one is claiming that advertisements, in the media or in print, turn hapless consumers into hypnotized automatons. Rather, the point is that suggestibility is a fundamental human personality characteristic that gets magnified in sometimes unusual ways in the social context called hypnosis, but which also operates in everyday settings including advertising campaigns that encourage conformity and stimulate desire. Consider the following example. In 2009 Dutch researchers showed that men who watched films and television commercials in which drinking occurred prominently, drank significantly more beer and wine during their viewing than others who watched programs and commercials that showed little or no alcohol consumption. On average those who watched the films in which drinking occurred drank approximately one-and-one half bottles more beer and wine than viewers who watched the other films. Although the suggestibility of individuals who participated in the study was not measured a medical report summarized the findings by saying: "watching movies and commercials could cause you to drink more alcohol, according to a new study on the power of suggestion." According to lead researcher Rutger Engles of Radboud University, "This is the first experimental study to show a direct effect of exposure to alcohol portrayals on TV on viewers' immediate drinking behavior."[9] Engles suggests that the research may indicate a need to restrict the advertising of alcohol and to introduce warnings in films. As Don Shenker of the group Alcohol Concern points out, "alcohol advertising and promotion on film and television usually present drinking as a positive social ritual, while leaving out the potential harm that drinking can cause."[10]

It is one thing to show that advertising affects behavior in a controlled laboratory setting. It would be more significant to show that it has adverse effects on the general population. Take cigarette smoking, one of the United States' and other nations' largest public health problems. Smoking leads to thousands of deaths annually from lung cancer and heart disease. Whatever it contributes positively to the economy is overshadowed by increased health care costs, lost work time, and personal tragedy. Why do people smoke? A typical smoker might say that he or she likes cigarettes, that they taste good, are relaxing, and that they help to control appetite and weight. For most smokers, however, smoking is not a conscious, rational choice. The fact is that the tobacco industry has made a concerted effort over many decades to establish and maintain cigarette smoking by means of subtle appeals to the emotions, and suggestions of which consumers may be consciously unaware.

In the United States cigarettes were not widely smoked before World War I. Most men preferred cigars, pipes, and chewing tobacco. Cigarettes were more convenient, however, and during the war the Army began to distribute them with soldiers' rations. American men became hooked. Women, on the other hand, were more of a problem. The war changed social mores, but women had to be convinced to take up smoking, especially outside of the home.

Enter the new field of public relations and advertising. In 1928 a young public relations man from New York named Edward Bernays was hired by the American Tobacco Company to promote smoking among American women. His first campaign focused on women's anxieties about weight. On Bernays' advice the company used the suggestion "Reach for a Lucky Instead of a Sweet" in its advertising, and sales of Lucky Strike cigarettes soared. The tobacco company, however, was not satisfied. Women were smoking in their homes, but they would not smoke in public. The company approached Bernays again and asked him to find a way to get women to smoke on the street. Bernays consulted the well-known psychoanalyst Dr. A. A. Brill who advised him that the emancipation of women had blurred the distinction between male and female roles. Women were doing the same work as men. Those who married had fewer children. Women wanted to do what men did. "Cigarettes," Brill concluded, "which are equated with men, become torches of freedom."[11]

What Bernays learned from Brill was that social contagion is not necessarily rational or conscious as sociologist David Phillips later noted in a study of suicide.[12] Phillips made a list of stories about suicide that appeared in the nation's top newspapers from the end of the 1940s to the end of the 1960s. He compared them to suicide statistics for the same period and found that suicides increased after stories about suicide appeared in the news. In a bizarre example that the author remembers from the period, radio stations in the San Francisco area began to publicize suicide jumps from the Golden Gate Bridge as the total number of such attempts began to approach 200. They stopped the practice when it became clear that their broadcasts were actually pushing some disturbed individuals into taking the plunge. Phillips argues that the decision by someone famous to commit suicide has the same effect. "It gives," he says, "other people, particularly those vulnerable to suggestion because of immaturity or mental illness, permission to engage in a deviant act as well."

Bernays was captivated by the phrase "torches of freedom," and he immediately turned it into a public relations campaign.[13] He sent invitations signed by his female secretary to 30 debutantes, inviting them to join her in combating prejudice and sexual stereotypes, by lighting "torches of freedom" during the 1929 Easter Parade on New York's fashionable Fifth Avenue. Bernays had a photographer ready to photograph several well dressed women lighting up as they left St. Patrick's Cathedral, and the photos appeared the next day in the major newspapers. The campaign was a huge success. American women began to smoke in large numbers. By the 1950s more than one-third of American women smoked cigarettes. Echoes of Bernay's slogan could be heard decades later when another brand of cigarettes advertised that women who smoked that brand had "come a long way baby."

Smoking by both men and women began to decline in the 1960s as the health dangers of smoking became apparent. Even today, however, almost one-quarter of all American women smoke and, interestingly, at least one study showed that women who smoked were significantly higher in hypnotic susceptibility than women who never smoked or who had quit.[14] Edward Bernays, more than any other individual, was responsible for getting American women hooked on cigarettes. He did it with the aid of psychoanalysis, and through suggestions that appealed to women's desires, conscious and unconscious, to be free. Edward Bernays was Sigmund Freud's nephew.

Our complex, consumer-based economy requires the constant creation and manipulation of desire to keep the system working, and a great industry has grown up, using the mass media and the power of suggestion, to perform that task. If desire were fundamentally harmless the harvest of such efforts might be bad taste and overstuffed garages but 10,000 years of human history reveal that desire is spawned by envy and envy leads to trouble. Trouble in a world of nuclear weapons is a problem.

6. The Manufacture of Envy

Many would argue that the diversity of views and news outlets, the free press, makes the occurrence of a totalitarian regime in the United States and other democratic nations unlikely, though some media critics argue that the American press is by no means free but rather controlled by and slanted in favor of wealthy corporate interests.

In any case the impact of suggestions presented by the American media over the past century has been predominantly commercial. For some people that is a fact to be celebrated in that it represents an extension of democracy into everyday life, the freedom to choose among competing goods and services. What some see as freedom, however, others view as the craven manipulation of the American psyche to produce a constant state of dissatisfaction and frustration based on envy. As author Betsy Cohen put it: "...the American dream is a movie run on the projector of envy. Our society not only encourages envy, it actually requires envy to maintain itself."[1] All of that has occurred since the creation of the mass media in the early 20th century.

In the years following the Civil War the United States developed an industrial infrastructure, primarily based on transportation, which eventually made it the most powerful economy on earth. Oil was discovered in Pennsylvania in 1859, two years before the war, opening the way decades later for the automotive industry. The eastern part of the nation was crisscrossed by navigable rivers and numerous canals which facilitated the movement of industrial goods. As American industry grew, traffic on these waterways surged. In 1860, for example, only about 100,000 tons of shipping passed through the Sault Ste. Marie canal between Lakes Superior and Huron. By 1901 that number had grown to 25 million tons.[2] It was primarily the railroads, however, upon which the post-war economy was built. In 1865, the year the war ended, there were 35,000 miles of railroad in the United States. By 1900 that number had increased to 175,000 miles.[3] In 1869 the transcontinental railroad, which was completed at Promontory Point, Utah by the hammering in of the Golden Spike, opened the West to a flood of migration and development. The railroads, which required large amounts of coal and steel, spurred the growth of those industries, spawned cattle production, and made possible the mass production of meat. The slaughter houses, in turn, produced leather for millions of pairs of shoes, and so on, and so on. By the turn of the 20th century the United States had an unprecedented capacity to produce goods, employ workers, and create wealth. There was only one problem. Most Americans did not know that they needed or wanted all of the goods that the industrial economy was capable of producing.

In 1790, when the first census was taken, the United States' population was approximately four million. Most Americans, approximately 90% of the total, farmed and were self-sufficient. They grew their own food, they built their own homes, and they sewed their own clothes. The consumer economy was very small. One hundred years later the population had grown fifteen-fold to approximately 63 million but approximately 43% of the population still farmed and their outlook remained conservative. Despite the excesses of the super rich, the so-called "Robber Barons," and rags-to-riches stories like those of Horatio Alger, Jr., most of the population, urban and agricultural, retained its commitment to an ethic that promoted self-sufficiency and encouraged men and women to accept their station in life and not to envy the position or possessions of others. Most Americans, including newcomers, expected to measure a better life in generations not quick fixes.

On January 1, 1892, for example, Annie Moore, a 15-year-old girl from Ireland, became the first immigrant to pass through Ellis Island in New York harbor. A statue of Annie and her brothers stands at the edge of the main pier in Cobh harbor from which they embarked. Thousands preceded her in the century before Ellis Island was opened, but it is Annie Moore and the 12 million immigrants who followed her before Ellis Island closed 62 years later who symbolize the pursuit of the American Dream. According to a well established story Annie headed west, settled in Texas, married, and had a successful life that one writer called a classic "go-West-young-woman tale..."[4] The problem is that the tale is not true. There was an Annie Moore in Texas at that time but she was not the immigrant who first stepped onto Ellis Island. The Annie who arrived in steerage on the steamship Nevada simply traveled the few miles from Ellis Island to Manhattan's Lower East Side where she lived the rest of her life. She led a "typical hardscrabble immigrant life," marrying a bakery clerk, bearing 11 children, of whom five survived to adulthood, and dying of heart failure in 1924 at the age of 47. Like most men and women Annie Moore, the icon of American immigration, died in obscurity. Like most immigrants she sacrificed herself to make a better life for her descendants, a typical American family that includes Irish, Jewish, Italian, and Scandinavian surnames. One guidebook says of her that Annie Moore came to America bearing little more than her dreams but stayed to help build a country enriched by diversity.[5]

In her book *Keeping up with the Joneses* Susan J. Matt recounts a magazine story that originally appeared in 1897. Annie Moore might have seen it. It concerned Mary, a pretty 16-year-old girl from a family of moderate circumstances. A school friend of Mary's named Esther had a beautiful pair of diamond earrings of which Mary was envious. She exclaimed to her mother that if only she had such a pair of earrings she would be totally happy. Her parents did not believe it, but they bought her the earrings in the hope that she would learn from them that "happiness does not consist in fine jewelry, but in a contended and cheerful spirit." In fact Mary soon tired of her earrings and began to envy the diamond bracelets of even wealthier young women. Her envy soon faded, however, because according to the story she was both "good and sensible." She realized that she could not have all that she wanted and that it was better to limit her desires. She asked her father to take the earrings back explaining that she realized she had been unhappy not because she had no diamonds but because she was "daily breaking the tenth commandment, and guilty of covetousness." Her selfless gesture made her parents weep with joy that Mary had learned such an important lesson.[6] It is ironic that some of the strongest supporters today of America's consumer-based capitalist economy are also fervent Christians who seem unfazed by the reality that the whole system violates one of the Ten Commandments.

Mary's sentiments expressed the dominant religious view in America in the 19ᵗʰ century concerning possessions. According to Matt clergy, magazine writers, and social reformers all tried to limit envy to preserve a conservative, hierarchical social order. They promoted the value of being content with one's lot in life instead of yearning for what one's neighbors had, views that reflected the centuries-long condemnation of envy by the Christian Church with which most 19ᵗʰ century Americans identified.

It is somewhat shocking, therefore, to find that advertisements at the beginning of the 20ᵗʰ century, just a few years after the fictional Mary returned her earrings, began to encourage envy! In 1909, for example, an advertisement in the *Saturday Evening Post* had the headline "All eyes envy the tailor-dressed man." It contained a picture of a man in a well-cut suit standing on a public conveyance as less well-dressed men seated around him gazed up in obvious admiration. In the century that followed Americans were inundated by a flood of advertisements designed not to provide information about products but to induce envy. Susan Matt points out that, beginning in the years just prior to World War I, "a far-flung group of advertisers, economists, sociologists, journalists, and consumers spread a new view of envy."[7] Its author was not God Almighty but the Almighty Dollar. In 1926 one essayist declared that the tenth commandment had been rewritten to state that: "Thou shalt not be outdone by thy neighbor's house, thou shalt not be outdone by thy neighbor's wife, nor his manservant, nor his car, nor anything – irrespective of its price or thine own ability – anything that is thy neighbor's."[8] Psychologist Erich Fromm wrote: "While in the nineteenth century the general tendency was to save, and not to indulge in expenses which could not be paid for immediately, the contemporary system is exactly the opposite."[9]

At the time many viewed this shift in ethics as appropriate. The American economic machine was turning out so many goods that envy seemed no longer to be a concern. There seemed to be plenty to go around. In fact many saw envy not as a wrong but as a socially constructive emotion that spurred economic growth and raised the standard of living for everyone. Consumer spending quickly accelerated well beyond the level of food, clothing, and shelter needed for survival. Social scientists have speculated as to why Americans over-consume. In her book *The Overspent American* (1998) Juliet Schor proposes that consumers set the standard for what they need to have not by observing those of similar status, but by comparing themselves with individuals who have higher incomes, in other words people whom they envy. Consumer satisfaction, she says, depends less on what a person has in an absolute sense than on socially formed aspirations and expectations, and these have been carefully planted and cultivated by the mass media.[10]

Guided by false images of wealth, and goaded by envy, many Americans have identified the pursuit of material goods possessed by others to be the pursuit of happiness, and many have been disappointed. Countless sources reveal envy not to be conducive to happiness but ultimately destructive. One of the strongest voices to make this point is Stanford University literary critic and historian René Girard whose theory of *mimesis* proposes that mimetic rivalry, a broader term that he uses instead of envy, leads ultimately to violence.[11] Girard believes that all desire is imitative or mimetic and thus endemic in human nature. In the past, Girard asserts, the ill will that accompanied envy was dissipated within a society by assigning blame to a scapegoat (e.g. Hitler blaming Jews for the German calamity of World War I). That mechanism he says, is no longer working because of the breakdown of social institutions such as religion that helped it to operate. The result is that violence and warfare are increasing, and, in Girard's view, approaching the apocalyptic.

Whether or not Girard is correct, there seems ample evidence that our envy-driven consumer economy is unstable, unsustainable, and potentially harmful. It is unstable because competition for material goods, or for the commodities to manufacture them, leads to violence. We have seen that over and over in national struggles to control petroleum, from Japan's efforts to stockpile oil in 1940 to the various wars in the Persian Gulf. It is unsustainable because the byproducts of consumption are polluting the environment and, according to many experts, producing global warming. It is harmful to the extent that men, women, and children are constantly frustrated by powerful suggestions given by the media to desire the unattainable. It is an old psychological principle that frustration begets aggression. Some of that aggression may be directed towards others, but in our highly structured society much of it gets directed inward resulting in sadness and worry. Indeed, the past 60 years or so, during which time the media have made industry the invisible government, Americans have drunk more alcohol than before, taken vastly more medicine for anxiety and depression, and supported a mental health care establishment of psychiatrists, psychologists, and family therapists that over the period has grown from almost nothing to be half again as large as the number of family doctors in the United States, and approximately 3.5

times larger than the number of Catholic priests. Many people, entranced by the media messages, cannot fathom that the consumer economy that brings us so much can be harmful. The evidence is there but, as the phrase goes, they are not connecting the dots.

Far from being a vast cornucopia that satisfies all wants the global economy is a pyramid of manufactured desire the apex of which, by design, can never be reached. Headlines in recent years have been full of stories about individuals (e.g. Bernard Madoff, Tiger Woods) who seemed to have everything one could want yet were unsatisfied.

Artificial desire

The cycle begins with the accumulation of stuff, so much stuff that many people earn their living by helping others to organize their closets and garages. According to a recent estimate by Mathis Wackernagel and William Rees, authors of *Our Ecological Footprint,* if everyone consumed at the level of the average North American, it would take four extra planets to provide the necessary resources to survive.[12] All of this material accumulation is the result of higher standards of living as reflected by consumer spending. At the beginning of the 20th century the average US household spent a bit more than $750 per year on goods and services. One hundred years later that amount was approximately $41,000 which, expressed in 1901 prices, would have bought more than $2000 worth of goods, a tripling of purchasing power. The United States has become a goods-oriented economy based on mass consumption spurred on by advertising and easy consumer credit. As a result, consumer spending has become the largest component of US gross domestic product, accounting for 70% of the US economy, and that makes most of us happy. We like our stuff, but, as with population growth and fossil fuel consumption, the unending spiral of desire has negative implications one of which is simply the sheer amount of waste that it generates.

Consider the largest object by volume ever constructed by human beings. Some might guess that it is the Great Wall in China, or the pyramids at Giza, but the correct answer is the Fresh Kills rubbish dump on Staten Island, New York.[13] Opened in 1948, it covered about four-and-one-half square miles. It is closed now but if it had stayed open it would eventually have grown to be the tallest structure on the East Coast. It was already higher than the Statue of Liberty when it shut down. At its operational peak 20 barges, each carrying 650 tons of trash and garbage dumped their cargo there every day. That was for one city. For the nation as a whole government figures reveal that the production of trash (solid waste) has grown much faster than the population. In 1960 the population of the United States was approximately 179 million people and the amount of solid waste generated by that population equaled approximately 88 million tons. Forty years later the population had grown by 57% to approximately 281 million people, but the amount of trash we generated grew 269% to 237 million tons. The good news is that much of that waste now gets recycled. In 1960 only six percent of the waste generated was recycled, whereas today that figure is about 44%.[14] Worrisome, however, are the increasing amounts of potentially harmful waste by-products that are polluting the air, water, and food supplies.

An alarming amount of pollution is generated just by pharmaceutical and personal care products. The United States Geological Services reports that steroids, prescription and nonprescription drugs such as acetaminophen and ibuprofen, antibiotics, hormones, and fragrances have been detected in water samples from streams susceptible to contamination. In 2008 a five-month-long inquiry by the Associated Press National Investigative Team found that drugs had been discovered in the drinking water supplies of 24 major metropolitan areas. Many communities do not test for the presence of drugs in drinking water, and those that do often fail to tell customers that they have found trace amounts of medications. They leach into the water from products discarded into landfills, from animal and industrial waste, from lotions released during swimming and bathing, and from expired or unused prescriptions that are flushed down the toilet.

Most people did not have to be coaxed into enjoying better health and longer life. When medical advances became available they used them. In a similar way when trains and cars became available people rode them. Despite the romance of the cowboy and all the wonderful stories in literature about noble horses, horses virtually disappeared from America's farms and streets in the 20 years following World War I. Human beings had always moved around. Cars and trains made it possible for them to go faster and farther. The desire for and accumulation of stuff was a different matter. As economist John Kenneth Galbraith remarked: "Few people at the beginning of the 19th century needed an adman to tell them what they wanted."[15] In an agricultural economy most wants are satisfied by what one produces oneself.

That is not true today when fewer than two percent of Americans live on farms.

The desire for new things is not self-evident or inevitable. Consumers have to be taught what to want and why they want it. One of the largest industries in the United States, for example, is beef production. American consumers love beef and eat 28 billion pounds of it per year produced from more than 96 million head of cattle but that does not mean that consumers will automatically buy every food item that the industry produces. The slaughtering of cattle produces a great deal of waste and by-product. Suppose you owned a butcher shop and decided that you would try to sell the waste protein found in cow bones, hooves, and connective tissues by setting up a large display of those body parts in your store. You probably would not have too many takers. That protein, however, called collagen, dissolved from the beef scraps, cooked, dried, flavored, and properly advertised is one of America's favorite fun foods, a staple in molded salads and desserts. It is, of course, gelatin. Our desire for it is not self-evident. It had to be taught.

The contagion of desire

Interestingly, one of the most comprehensive studies of how desire is acquired took place on the farm in what is called diffusion research.[16] The classic study concerned the pattern of adoption of hybrid seed corn by American farmers in the 1930s. Guided by the work of Darwin and Mendel, agronomists began to cross breed strains of corn early in the 20th century, and they soon produced hybrids that were stronger and more resistant to drought and disease than native varieties. They also yielded more corn per acre. Traditional seeds produced about 35-40 bushels per acre, whereas the new hybrids produced 150 bushels. There was only one drawback: hybrids are sterile. They do not generally reproduce. That meant that self-reliant Midwestern farmers, who previously provided for the next year's crop by holding back some of their best corn from market, would now be totally dependent upon manufacturers for seed. The first hybrid corn was introduced by Pioneer Hi-Breds, of Des Moines, Iowa, in 1926. Ten years later almost all American corn was produced from hybrid seed, one of the most remarkable revolutions ever to take place in agriculture. How that revolution took place was studied and documented by Bryce Ryan and Neal C. Gross of Iowa State University.

In 1939 Bryce Ryan was a young professor at Iowa State with a degree in sociology from Harvard. He had studied diffusion in anthropology as a graduate student and endeavored to apply his studies to the adoption of hybrid corn. The subject was one of immense importance to the nation. Increased corn production helped to lift the United States out of the Great Depression and contributed vitally to the war effort that followed. In the summer of 1941 Ryan hired Neal Gross, a graduate student, to interview farmers living in two small Iowa communities located about 50 miles west of Ames, where the university was located. Gross used a structured questionnaire that enabled his interviews to be analyzed quantitatively. He asked farmers about their age, level of education, farm size, income, travel, and readership of farm magazines, and he later correlated these scores with the year in which the farmer adopted the hybrid. The results showed that the farmers' rate of adoption followed an "S-shaped" curve. In the first few years only a few planted the new corn. Then, adoption shot up by 40% over the next three years, after which it leveled off again. Ryan and Gross recognized that the new idea had spread as a sort of contagion. One person "caught the bug," after which more and more became affected until finally it had spread through the whole community. Ryan and Gross concluded that: "There is no doubt but that the behavior of one individual in an interacting population affects the behavior of his fellows. Thus, the demonstrated success of hybrid seed on a few farms offers new stimulus to the remaining ones."[17] The diffusion of an innovation is a social process based on social modeling. When one person adopts a new idea others may quickly follow.

In his book *The Tipping Point* Malcolm Gladwell refines the concept of diffusion by pointing out that whether a new idea or product will catch on depends on three "rules of epidemics," which he calls the "law of the few," "the stickiness factor," and "the power of context."[18] The law of the few refers to the fact that those who spread a new idea or use a new product are not equal. Some are more effective at making connections and selling an idea to the public than others. The stickiness factor refers to the ability of a new idea or product to catch the attention of the public in the midst of the cacophony of messages to which we are all subjected daily. Americans are inundated by thousands of advertisements, by one estimate more than 3000 per day, which are part of a verbal tsunami of 100,000 words to which the average American is exposed daily, more than half of which are presented on radio or television.[19] Sticky ideas are ones that hold the viewer's or listener's attention. The power of context derives from what psychologists call the *fundamental attribution error* which means the greater likelihood that most people will

THE MANUFACTURE OF ENVY

attribute an individual's behavior to his or her character, rather than to the situation in which it takes place.

To illustrate the law of the few Gladwell cites the story of Paul Revere's famous ride to warn the American colonists that British troops were marching on Lexington and Concord to arrest colonial leaders and seize their stores of arms. As a result of his ride the colonial militia defeated the British in what became the opening battle of the American Revolution. What many people forget, or never knew, is that another patriot named William Dawes also rode that night but few people heeded his warning. Dawes was simply not well known, and he did not know key people in the various communities that he needed to alert. Revere, on the other hand, was a gregarious and sociable person, what Gladwell calls a "connector." He knew which people to seek out and because they knew him they listened to him.

From its beginnings in agriculture diffusion research has been applied to the adoption of innovations as diverse as electric cars, kindergarten, laptop computers, refrigerators, smoking cessation, cell phones and many others. Two things have to happen before someone adopts or desires a new thing: he or she has to know about it and must be persuaded to try it. That, in turn, depends on the innovation's relative advantages compared to the existing way of doing things, its compatibility with existing values, its complexity, how easily others who are respected can be observed using it, and how easy it is to try. If something new is in wide supply it can be adopted with benefit and little disruption to the society. Many innovations, however, involve finite commodities that lead to competition and potential violence among members of a group. For most of human history the process of social comparison that leads to the desire for some object took place by the direct observation of friends and neighbors. For about the last 100 years, however, most, desires have been created artificially by techniques of mass persuasion.

The "good life"

American children receive an extensive education in what constitutes the "good life" from the media and from friends who have in turn been influenced by the media. In New York half a dozen girls age three-and-one-half to seven gathered not long ago at the bubble gum colored pedicure lounge of Dashing Diva to celebrate one girl's birthday with manicures, pedicures, and mini-makeovers.[20] Before they were through they received light makeup and body art that included glitter-applied stars, lightning bolts, and hearts. The makeover party was part of a trend by cosmetic companies and retailers to transform six to nine year-old girls into sophisticated beauty consumers before they are out of elementary school, a trend that some call KGOY, "kids getting older younger." According to the research marketing firm Experian, a 2007 study found 55% of six to nine year-old girls said they used lip gloss or lipstick and nearly two-thirds said that they used nail polish.

Coached from an early age such consumers easily mature into teens obsessed with appearances. The standards to which they can aspire 10 years down the road were embodied in the MTV reality series *My Super Sweet Sixteen,* which aired 2005-2008. In each episode the spoiled son or daughter of exceedingly rich parents prepared for his or her coming out party. The parties took place in elaborately decorated and expensive venues to which the teen might be brought in a stretch limo, or a Roman chariot, or carried on a throne by the burly arms of shirtless bearers. There the teen and 200 or more of his or her invited guests enjoyed a lavish party with live music by the most popular bands. In one episode a boy spent $250,000 on jewelry for his party. In another the birthday girl, clearly an honors graduate of the KGOY school, prepared by getting an $800 manicure with real diamond inlays.[21] At the end of the party the teen often received a "surprise" gift of an expensive luxury car from his or her parents. The cost of such parties ran into the hundreds of thousands of dollars or more.

In the United States more than 57 million school age children and teenagers spend about $100 billion each year of their own and their family's money on sweets, food, drinks, video and electronic products, toys, games, movies, sports, clothes and shoes.[22] They also influence family spending decisions worth another $165 billion on food, household items like furniture, electrical appliances and computers, vacations, the family car and other spending. One study, from the 1990s, estimated that children influenced $9 billion worth of car sales, sometimes actually picking out the family car.

To aid them in their choices American companies invest more than $270 billion per year in advertising,[23] almost $1000 per year to influence the buying habits of every man, woman and child in the United States, more than half as much as is spent on all public school education. In many ways advertising constitutes a second educational system, part of the "invisible government," almost as large as, and perhaps even more powerful in its influence, than the formal educational system. One of the most powerful advertising media is television, and Americans families spend as much time watching TV, on average, as they spend at work or at school. In 2006, the Nielsen Media Research company reported that television viewing by American households averaged eight hours, 14 minutes per day, an increase over previous years despite competition from other media such as iPods, cell phones, and streaming video. Among those showing the greatest gains in viewing time were children and teenagers, especially teenage girls. The consequences of such artificially stimulated consumption remain unknown and poorly regulated. Agencies that focus on deceptive advertising, for example, have budgets totaling only about one-thousandth as much as what is spent on advertising itself.

Americans not only spend heavily for tangible goods, many spend real money for imaginary goods that only exist in the virtual world of computer games. Thousands of people in the US and elsewhere exchange real money every day for virtual, that is nonexistent, real estate and goods such as a beautiful, but imaginary, palm-studded beachfront property for $550 an acre. By one estimate more than $5 million changed hands in 2006 in one game alone called Second Life. Some play the game to make a profit in the real world. Other people play to achieve status in the virtual world that eludes them in the real one. In one game a delivery truck driver paid 750 real dollars, a significant sum for him, to purchase a luxury home in the virtual world that he could never have afforded in real life. When asked why he did it he explained that it only seemed right to own a nice home in which to entertain his virtual friends.[24] Some critics have asserted that what millions of Americans are embracing is not the American Dream but the "American daydream."

Many people believe that happiness can be defined by some degree of affluence or comfort, but psychological studies of human satisfaction suggest that that is not the case. Government statistics show that from the year 1950 to the year 2000 the buying power of the average American doubled, yet the percentage of Americans who rated themselves as "very happy" remained constant at about 30%.[25] As one psychologist concluded, "Economic growth in affluent countries has provided no apparent boost to morale or social well-being."[26]

Two principles help to explain why material happiness is relative. The first is what psychologists call adaptation level. We evaluate our current situation in terms of what we have experienced in the past. To someone who has been earning $50,000 per year a $25,000 raise might seem wonderful, but to someone who was earning $100,000 per year, a reduction to $75,000 might be devastating. Similarly, to someone who lives in the San Francisco Bay Area a December day with temperatures in the low 50°s F seems cold, whereas to a visitor arriving from Minnesota it may seem quite mild. According to a second principle, that of relative deprivation, we judge our current level of happiness not by what we have attained but by what others possess. In other words a desired goal, such as a salary of $75,000 per year, will never seem like enough if we find out that all the co-workers to whom we compare ourselves earn more. In his book *The Conquest of Happiness* philosopher Bertrand Russell noted that humanity can never get away from envy by means of success alone, because "there will always be in history or legend some person even more successful than you are."[27]

Unintended consequences

In recent years some voices have begun to caution that improvements in the human condition are producing negative unintended consequences. The term, first coined by sociologist Robert K. Merton, refers to the unforeseen side effects of any action. Progress has come at a price and we are paying it. Consider just one cost: noise. Machines make noise and our environment is full of them. Few urban dwellers ever experience the quiet of a machine-free environment. Listen to the noises around you right now. Turn off the television, radio, iPod and other devices. Is there a hum from the fluorescent lights in your room? Turn them off and hear the difference. Now pull the plug on the refrigerator, turn down the heat or air conditioning and begin to notice the noises outside your room: the passing bus, the drone of a distant airplane, the muffled roar of a nearby freeway. Scientists tell us that the background noises of nature such as the rustling of leaves, measured on the decibel scale, are one hundred to one thousand times less noisy than a busy street corner. That means that the sound pressures that impinge upon our ears on a daily basis are 100 to 1000 times greater, on average, than the sounds to which the ears were adapted by nature. Even worse, exposure to highly amplified noises, such as a rock band at close range, may be one million times greater than the background sounds of nature. One might expect that prolonged exposure to such noise would damage the ears and one would be right. In 1962 Dr. Samuel Rosen, a hearing specialist, published the results of hearing tests he conducted among Mabaan tribesmen in Sudan where at the time there were few machines. He tested the hearing of boys, young men, and old men and found virtually no hearing loss among the Mabaan as a result of age, whereas such loss is common among urban males.[28]

The media are filled with warnings about other hidden costs of material progress including crowding, pollution, greenhouse gases, and nuclear proliferation. As author Tony Judt, put it: "The American pursuit of wealth, size, and abundance – as material surrogates for happiness – is aesthetically unpleasing and ecologically catastrophic."[29] Most alarming is that the changes wrought by technology over the past century have not been incremental. They have been on a scale never before seen, levels of magnitude that would have been unimaginable a few centuries ago. The leap in destructive power, for example, from cannons to nuclear bombs is unlike anything in history, and the side effects of other technologies have been equally great. Governmental officials, scientists, and concerned citizens are just beginning to grasp the global scope and interrelatedness of these changes. Many are shocked by what they see. Curiously, the media that report such events fail to report that the media also cause unintended consequences as far reaching as the lengthening of life and the warming of the environment.

Media pollution

We think of pollution as an unintended consequence of physical science technology, but the social sciences, particularly the media, also produce pollution. In some ways this "psychological" pollution is the worst type because the pollutants are not molecules or particles but human beings.[30] At one time, for example, intelligence tests that required an understanding of English were

95

administered to school children who did not speak English well and who therefore scored poorly. That led to some children from minority communities being labeled as mentally disabled and subsequently denied educational opportunities who in fact were not disabled at all. More recently critics have argued that college aptitude tests, themselves a kind of intelligence test, are based on skills and knowledge that favor the white middle-class majority. Minority applicants, who may be highly successful in their own cultures, may do poorly on the tests and find themselves excluded from certain educational opportunities. Like unburned hydrocarbons these individuals become a sort of human smog adrift and potentially harmful in the larger social environment.

Of all the social science technologies mass persuasion creates the largest and most caustic pollution. Edward Bernays and others believed that the manipulation of public opinion was essential to the functioning of a complex society such as the United States. Since about 1920 that manipulation has taken place, was effected by means of the mass media, became amplified by the introduction of television after World War II, and was successful, especially with children, because it tapped into the same power of suggestion that characterizes hypnosis. The result has been a remarkable increase in personal and household wealth brought about by envy and a compulsion to buy, along with a plethora of psychological problems caused by artificial desires that can, by design, never be fulfilled.

Proponents of the consumer-driven economy do not see a problem. They say that to the extent that the consumption of material goods equals economic growth everyone benefits. There may be problems with waste and by-products but they are manageable and we are working on solutions for them. They overlook something important. Although human history has always been violent the period since The Renaissance, during which the greatest material progress has taken place, has been particularly violent. Deaths as a result of warfare have been increasing worldwide for five centuries. If progress has brought prosperity it has also brought destruction. Moreover, in the past 100 years, the age of the consumer economy, there has been an implosion of inwardly directed violence in the form of unhappiness, depression and anxiety that have, in turn, spawned the production of vast amounts of medication to dull the pain of modern living.

Some might claim that, although there have been vicious wars between nation states, the survivors within those states (e.g. Britain during the 19th Century; America in the 20th Century) by and large have been prosperous and happy. Many would disagree. Colonialism and industrialization raised standards of living for many but also created great imbalances in wealth combined with what many have viewed as an impoverishment of the soul. Charles Dickens wrote of such conditions in Britain as did Thomas Hardy somewhat later and many others. In the United States social critics at the turn of the 20th century, such as Upton Sinclair, Lincoln Steffens, and Ida Tarbell, decried the inhuman working conditions of American industry. Mid-century writers described the drabness of middle-class corporate life with such books as David Riesman's *The Lonely Crowd* (1950) and William H. Whyte's *The Organization Man* (1956). In the 1960s many children of America's victors in World War II abandoned the "good life" to become Hippies and to initiate a vast social movement that became known as the Counter Culture.

These voices have brought about some improvements in social conditions for ordinary men and women, but the underlying problem remains. The economic system in which we live is founded on dissatisfaction. In theory that should lead people to work harder to make more money and thus to advance the whole system. In practice it has resulted in endemic anxiety and depression among individuals, as evidenced by the explosive growth of psychology, and ever more dangerous envy and competition between nations. Beginning with childhood, the media, using psychological techniques, create desires for a lifestyle that few, if any, can achieve. Under the stress of working to fulfill these manufactured desires men and women break down, psychologists patch their psychic wounds, and they re-enter the vortex. The cycle is complete but it is not stable. Materialistic, dissatisfied and ultimately violent: if these are the earmarks of the perfect society that stands as a model for future human development there is much to worry about.

7. The Pathology of Envy

Everyone recognizes the vicious evil that was Nazism and the role of the mass media in creating and sustaining it, but even if the same forces made and maintained the post-war consumer economy, is that a bad thing? We said earlier that the success of mass persuasion depends on the ability of the media to use suggestions to create envy. Envy is ancient, as old as the human species. If Gabriel Tarde was right that imitation is the foundation of all social living then envy is inevitable. The problem is that envy implies not only the desire to possess something but also the desire that other people should not possess it. Economists recognize that all people gauge their well being by the standards of others, and that is not necessarily a bad thing. In his comprehensive overview of the topic of envy in 1966 German sociologist Helmut Schoeck wrote that a society of equals without envy was impossible and that envy was necessary for economic and social progress. He cautioned, however, that "to keep a society going, and to ensure that essential social processes take place, only a minimum of envy in that society's members is requisite. Envy in excess of that minimum is a surplus which can, as often as not, be 'digested' by the social system, but it will certainly do more harm than good..."[1] Envy, in other words, is ultimately destructive a point made repeatedly by René Girard in his writing about mimetic violence.

American economist and social critic Thorstein Veblen theorized that all economic life involves both imitation and predation. If one person acts to improve his or her status relative to another the other, of necessity,

99

must decline in status, and the primary weapon used to inflict the decline is material wealth. In his book *The Theory of the Leisure Class,* first published in 1899, Veblen pointed out that both rich and poor tried to impress others and gain social advantage by means of what he called "conspicuous consumption." The desire for things, in other words, can be both comparative and destructive. Another 19th century author, Charles Mackay, made that point with stories of various mass phenomena in which contagious desire led to disaster.[2] They include the Tulip Mania in early 17th century Holland and the English South-Sea Bubble in the 18th century.

Tulips, which originally came to Europe from Istanbul, were so prized by the Dutch for their beauty and uniqueness that a market developed in futures contracts for tulip bulbs. The value of these contracts increased rapidly to as much as 10 times the annual income of a skilled worker. In 1636 one person offered 12 acres of building land for one tulip bulb. In time the market crashed and large fortunes were lost. "Men," Mackay said, "think in herds."

The South-Sea bubble was a run on stocks that has a more modern ring. It began in 1711 as a government attempt to pay war debts. The debt, amounting to 10 million pounds sterling was assumed by a private company of merchants who in return received from the government a guaranteed interest rate of six percent for a period of time and a monopoly on trade to coasts of South America. The alleged riches of the trade were estimated to be so great, and the initial profits so lavish, that a furious market grew up in shares of all sorts of companies. Virtually any new business offering stock, no matter how obliquely related to trade, became immediately oversubscribed.

One shameless entrepreneur even advertised: "A company for carrying on an undertaking of great advantage, but nobody knows what it is."[3] He issued 5000 shares for sale at an initial price of 100 pounds each which could be secured with a deposit of two pounds per share. In return he promised each subscriber 100 pounds per year per share. When he opened his London sales office he was beset by crowds who pressed him to take their deposits all day. By three o'clock in the afternoon he had deposits for no less than 1000 shares, disappeared that evening for the Continent, and was never heard of again. As for the South Seas Company itself the market eventually crashed with disastrous losses for many, and an anguished public outcry led to trials for several of the principals that resulted in fines and confinement in the Tower of London.

Boom and bust, greed and envy, smash and grab: generation after generation of human beings lurch through the same cycle of desire and destruction. It is not that we have not been warned. Minatory accounts of the consequences of envy, such as those of Adam and Eve and Cain and Abel, form some of the oldest stories in human literature, especially within the Abrahamic religious tradition. Whether or not you believe that these stories are factual, they are central to the religious traditions of Jews, Christians, and Muslims who constitute approximately half of the world's population. In the Judeo-Christian Scriptures [Genesis 2: 15 25] Adam and Eve were created by God to live in the earthly Garden of Eden. According to the Quran [2:35] Adam and Eve resided in paradise until their transgression caused them to be cast down onto the earth. Otherwise the basic story is the same: God/Allah told Adam and Eve not to eat fruit from the forbidden tree, that is, not to envy the wisdom of God.

Adam and Eve disobeyed and were expelled from paradise, whether it was on earth or in heaven.

Of all the stories that might have constituted the first story of humanity for so many people why is this one at the beginning? The first story could have been a fertility story: "Adam and Eve loved one another, were happy, and begot many children," or it could have been a story of the hardships of earthly survival, but it is about envy. Adam and Eve wanted what God had. The answer is that from the most ancient times, and through the most sacred writings, human beings have recognized that envy is the most fundamental of all human motives and the primary source of all problems.

According to John Milton's great epic *Paradise Lost*[4]*,* envy comes directly from Satan the author of all evil who was alienated from God because Satan envied Jesus. Milton writes:

> "Who first seduced them to that foul revolt?
>
> Th'infernal Serpent! He it was, whose guile
>
> Stirred up with Envy and Revenge, deceived
>
> The Mother of Mankind..."
>
> "With envy against the Son of God, that day
>
> Honoured by his great Father, and proclaimed
>
> Messiah King anointed, could not bear
>
> Thro' pride that sight, and thought himself impaired."
> (1.34-37)

Perhaps the most graphic account of the consequences of envy is provided In the *Divine Comedy* by 14th century author Dante Alighieri who defined envy as the "love of one's own good perverted to a desire to deprive other men of theirs." According to Dante, because the envious rejoiced in seeing their rivals brought low, their punishment in purgatory was to have their eyes sewn shut with iron wire, the tears squeezed out of their closed eyes.

Dante's punishment reflected a long history that connects envy and the eyes. Throughout history people in many cultures believed that envy was expressed through the "evil eye," a malicious glance born of envy that had the power to harm. References to the evil eye can be found 5000 years ago in the cuneiform texts of the Sumerians, Babylonians, and Assyrians. In her book *The Snow White Syndrome: All About Envy* Betsy Cohen points out that in many parts of the world today people shun compliments because they expose the person to the dangers of envy.[5] Mothers in India, Egypt, the Middle East, and southern Asia, she says would be as unlikely to show a new baby in public as an American mother would be to expose a new baby to a contagious disease. Societies that fear the evil eye have many folk precautions to guard against it including hanging strips of garlic or red chilies around the door to one's house, painting the entrance with red paint, wearing charms and amulets, reciting certain incantations, and in the case of women in India wearing the *bindi*, a red spot in the center of the forehead to ward off evil. Use of the bindi is not restricted to Hindus. It is also used in Southeast Asia by Christian and Muslim women.

Envy and the end of the world

Not everyone views envy as simply a problem of individual morality. As noted earlier, Stanford University historian and literary critic René Girard believes that envy is endemic in human nature, that it is insatiable, and that it will lead inevitably to apocalyptic violence. Girard talks of mimetic desire out of which, he believes, grow passions that include "jealousy, envy, covetousness, resentment, rivalry, contempt and hatred."[6] For Girard mimesis, or the tendency to imitate the behavior of others, is the defining human quality and the basis for human motivation. He views all human desire as mediated, or mimetic, meaning that individual wants come not from intrinsic preferences but from social comparisons.

Girard's views derived originally from his study of literature and later from anthropology. His analyses of the works of Proust, Dostoevsky and others revealed common structural properties or psychological laws that transcended the individual differences among various novels. Fundamental to this discovery is what Girard called the mimetic nature of desire, classically two men wanting the same woman or two women wanting the same man. Mimetic desire leads to mimetic rivalry which is inherently socially destabilizing and leads to violence. Throughout history, according to Girard, various societies controlled mimetic rivalry through religion and by designating a scapegoat for the society's problems whose sacrifice tended to restore the society to equilibrium. Girard's studies, however, have revealed to him that for the past several hundred years, the modern era, an epidemic of mimetic desire has gradually overwhelmed the social structures that earlier groups had used to defuse violence. In his book *Violence Unveiled: Humanity at the Crossroads*

Gil Bailie, a Girard disciple, points out that "even as the West turned its economic dynamos with mediated desire, it grew daily less nimble at using the scapegoating apparatus to convert the mimetic aggravations that resulted into healthy camaraderie."[7]

The statistics of warfare over the past four centuries support Girard's and Bailie's view if one looks at number of deaths caused by battle, disease and famine in wars that resulted in one million or more deaths, but not as a percentage of world population which shows a decrease. (Table 7.1)

Table 7.1

Deaths as a Percentage of World Population in Wars with at Least One Million Deaths[8]

	Total Deaths	Percentage of World Population
1600-1699	41,500,000	5.9
1700-1799	None Listed	
1800-1899	123,000,000	1.8
1900-present	167,900,000	0.7

The figures are an approximation based on the conflicts chosen for analysis, estimates of casualties, and whether those estimates include deaths from disease and famine. Using different data others have come to the same point: that war deaths have decreased over the past four centuries as a percentage of world population although technology has increased war's deadliness. It remains to be seen if the relative plateau in worldwide violence that has occurred during the past half century represents a trend, as some suggest, or only a time out before another round of even more devastating violence. René Girard is pessimistic. He believes that nothing now exists to stop the uncontrolled expansion of violence in the world. Nuclear weapons which some experts assert are keeping the world at peace in fact place us at the precipice of total destruction. For the first time, Girard, asserts, humanity is confronted "with a perfectly straight-forward and even scientifically calculable choice between total destruction and the total renunciation of violence."[9]

Girard is widely regarded and respected throughout the world. A member of the Académie Française, his writings have attracted a wide following. They are promulgated by the Colloquium on Violence and Religion (COV&R) through conferences and its journal *Contagion*. Two factors, however, limit Girard's influence: (1) his theory has not been much applied to understanding the worst aspects of scapegoating and violence in the modern age, such as the Holocaust; and (2) it has not meshed very well with the studies of behavioral and social scientists who are also interested in envy and its relation to violence. A search of the COV&R database, for example, produces no citations for such terms as "Nazis," "Hitler," "Anne Frank," or "Buchenwald" out of the hundreds and hundreds of books and articles that have been written about Girard's theory. Only four citations refer to the term "Jews" none of which directly relates to the events surrounding World War II, and the term "holocaust" produces only eight citations, six of which directly concern Nazi treatment of the Jews.

Psychologists, historically, have been more interested in jealousy, which refers to the loss of a desired object, than with envy. In the past 20 years or so, however, psychologists interested in social comparison theory (e.g. Salovey, 1991)[10] have written extensively about envy. None, however, refers to the work of Girard or his followers who, for their part, generally do not cite the behavioral science literature. The COV&R database, for example, contains no references to "social comparison theory," which explains how individuals evaluate their opinions and desires by comparing themselves to others, or to Leon Festinger the social psychologist who proposed it in 1954, seven years before Girard's first writings about mimesis in *Deceit, Desire and the Novel* (1961).

Despite the lack of connectedness between Girard and the social sciences his influence among academics is considerable. Girard forces us to confront the universality and centrality of violence in human life and the ubiquity of scapegoating as a mechanism for controlling violence. He traces these back through writings and anthropological evidence from earliest historical times to the present. Contrary to the sanguine view of humanists who look for peace through human progress, Girard is not optimistic. A devout Roman Catholic he believes firmly that we are moving rapidly toward a bad end and that human salvation can only be found through faith. The failure of Girard and his followers to communicate with social scientists of similar interests, and vice versa, is a classic but regrettable example of the immiscibility of the sciences and humanities, an example of the wide gap between what C. P. Snow called the Two Cultures.[11]

Not everyone agrees that violence is spiraling out of control. In his book *The Better Angels of Our Nature*[17] psychologist Steven Pinker argues that globalization of trade and education have provided individuals, especially

107

in the West, with a world view that emphasizes reason and reduces violence. He points out that the world currently is relatively peaceful and, for the most part, one would have to agree. It remains to be seen whether Pinker's optimism about the future is justified. There have been many wars in the post-WWII era but they have been regional and limited in destructiveness. Is that because humanity has evolved intellectually, or is it because we have simply not found a way to use nuclear weapons without retaliation and mutual destruction?

Two programs appeared on television not long ago on the same day. One concerned "Kokura's luck:" the fact that the city of Kokura, Japan unknowingly avoided atomic annihilation in August, 1945 because of bad weather which diverted American bombers to Nagasaki. The pilot of the plane that dropped the second atomic bomb was Major Charles Sweeny who later vigorously defended the use of the bomb as necessary to avoid the greater slaughter of an invasion. He also hoped that the power of the bomb would act as a deterrent to its ever being used again. On the program, one of his sons noted that Sweeny's optimistic view had been proved right, so far anyway. During the Cold War American national security was based on a strategy of Mutually Assured Destruction which posited that neither the United States nor the Soviet Union would attack the other if the result would be its own annihilation. The attacks of 9/11, however, showed that small numbers of terrorists can commit acts of great violence against which there is little defense.

The second program concerned US Government plans for response to a nuclear terrorist attack on Washington, DC. It described the immediate and longer term effects of a small weapon that might be smuggled into the country in a box or piece of luggage. If detonated a few blocks from the White House such a bomb would destroy everything within a radius of about one-half mile, but outside of that blast zone, the report concluded, such a nuclear explosion would be "relatively survivable." In other words, US defense planners are preparing for future nuclear blasts on US soil that may kill tens of thousands of people and destroy vast amounts of property, against which the strategy of mutual destruction may not apply. Given concerns about nuclear programs in Iran and North Korea as well as the problems of tracking fissile material that may have gotten "lost," it seems clear that Pinker's rosy view of the future is not the last word.

A sick society

Envy may be inevitable in human life but that does not mean that a society that promotes envy and defines human worth in terms of material possessions is either stable or good. Just as an individual person can become sick so can an entire society. The world witnessed such an event during the Nazi era in Germany. As the German psychoanalyst and philosopher Erich Fromm said: "The fact that millions of people share the same vices does not make these vices virtues, the fact that they share so many errors does not make the errors to be truths, and the fact that millions of people share the same forms of mental pathology does not make these people sane."[13] For Herbert Marcuse, author of *One Dimensional Man*, post-war technological society, the parameters of which are established by the media, is also totalitarian though less outwardly violent. He calls ours "an advanced society which makes scientific and technical progress into an instrument of domination."[14] He considers this society to be irrational, pathogenic, and ultimately unstable because its oppressiveness will eventually cause men and women to seek "new dimensions of human realization" that cannot be contained within existing social institutions. We see Marcuse's predictions playing out perhaps in the environmental movement and the strident debate over global warming.

Frustration and aggression

Social and behavioral scientists have long been interested in the connection between envy and violence. William James (1842-1910), one of the founders of modern scientific psychology, summed up the problem of violence this way: "In many respects man is the most ruthlessly ferocious of beasts. As with all gregarious animals, 'two souls,' as Faust says, 'dwell within his breast,' the one of sociability and helpfulness, the other of jealousy and antagonism to his mates...Constrained to be a member of a tribe, he still has a right to decide, as far as in him lies, of which other members of the tribe shall consist. Killing off a few obnoxious ones may often better the chances of those that remain. And killing off a neighboring tribe from whom no good thing comes, but only competition, may materially better the lot of the whole tribe. Hence the gory cradle, the *bellum omnium contra omnes*,[15] in which our race was reared; hence the fickleness of human, ties, the ease with which the foe of yesterday becomes the ally of today, the friend of today the enemy of tomorrow."[16]

Human beings have developed the most complex social relationships of any species on earth but at the same time retain the primal instincts that impel all other creatures, individually, to survive. One of the most basic is for an organism to lash out with aggression when blocked

110

from attaining something that it wants. The link between blocked desire, frustration, and aggression has been the subject of extensive psychological analysis and research. William McDougall (1871-1938), for example, an early comparative psychologist who studied instinct and motivation across species, asserted that aggression, which he called the "instinct of combat," was a direct consequence of "obstructionism" which he used synonymously with frustration. Moreover he noted that the amount of aggression was a function of the degree of frustration. He said: "Whenever we look at the animal kingdom, the same rule seems to obtain: in general terms, the stronger the impulse at work in an animal, the more readily is the angry combative behavior evoked by any obstruction from other creatures."[17]

McDougall's observations supported what Sigmund Freud's patients reported in psychoanalysis. A woman who was frustrated by her husband, for example, revealed death wishes to Freud directed toward her child whom she had with the husband. In another case a man who was frustrated in his professional life recounted a dream in which he did away with his rival. Freud, in his early writings, considered the pleasure motive, that is, the tendency to seek pleasure and to avoid pain, to be the basic mechanism of mental functioning. He believed that when pleasure seeking or pain avoidance was blocked aggression occurred which he believed to be a primordial reaction.

Although Freud, as a medical doctor, thought of his work as science his reports were anecdotal and his theories difficult to test. In the early 20th century American psychologists attempted to make psychology strictly empirical. They took the view that only events that could be openly measured, such as learned responses, should fall within the domain of psychology. One of the leading centers for the study of learning in the 1920s and 1930s was Yale University where various psychologists applied the behaviorists' demand for scientific rigor to studies of human behavior as well as to principles of learning in other species. An important development in that direction was the founding of the Institute of Human Relations in 1929 which, 10 years later, published a book that recast some of Freud's insights into scientific psychology. It was called *Frustration and Aggression,* authored by John Dollard, Leonard Doob, Neal Miller, Hobart Mowrer, and Robert Sears.[18]

Dollard, et al. did not confine their research to laboratory studies but rather studied human social behavior in the broadest sense. According to Freud when an individual was prevented either from seeking pleasure or avoiding pain the result was frustration and ultimately aggression. From these principles Dollard et al. derived testable hypotheses that stated, for example, that the strength of aggression should vary with the strength of the frustrated response, the degree of interference with it, and the number of times that the frustration had occurred. Many psychologists tested such hypotheses in the laboratory where some well defined response of a cat or a rat could be interfered with and studied. Dollard, et al. showed that their hypotheses could also be confirmed in real-world settings. Writing toward the end of the Great Depression, Hovland and Sears for example, studied the effect of economic conditions on aggressive behavior.[19] In particular they hypothesized that bad economic conditions would interfere with normal goal-seeking and result in violence. To support their point they correlated crop

THE PATHOLOGY OF ENVY

values with the annual number of lynchings in 14 Southern states for the years 1882-1930 and found that lynchings (aggression) increased as economic frustration increased.[20] In a similar way D. S. Thomas found a positive relationship between poor economic conditions and property crimes that involved violence.[21]

Dollard, et al. were aware that their writings had social and political significance. They noted that Marx's doctrine of class struggle and the nature of the state depended in part on the frustration-aggression principle. Marx reasoned that the proletariat (workers) were oppressed because they were treated as a commodity and because the use of machinery and the division of labor had stripped their jobs of all individual character and consequently of all "charm."[22] The result was aggression that proceeded, in theory, from struggles by individual workers against a factory owner, to struggles by all the workers within a factory, to the formation of unions, to outright violence all of which result in the ruling class exerting the power of the state to control labor. As a result of the factory workers' loss of pride, exploitation by their employers, economic crises, and state-sponsored repression Dollard, et al. concluded that workers developed profound frustrations that led "inevitably to aggression and eventually, according to the Marxian prediction, to the triumph of the oppressed class."

The success of labor movements in the United States during the 20th century, the changing nature of work, and the global vitality of capitalism have preempted some of Marx's predictions. Nevertheless, countless Americans still work at meaningless jobs from which they derive no satisfaction in a highly controlled society awash in images of violence. Rather than blaming the boss or the system for their lack of success and lack of satisfaction in life, they blame themselves. The result is violence turned inward. Dollard, et al., note that self-castigation may be a displaced form of inhibited direct aggression and that "not only verbal abuse but also physical injury and even neurotic symptoms of illness can be expressions of aggression directed toward the self."[23]

Not all psychologists accept the hypothesis that frustration produces aggression. Indeed, Dollard, et al. did not assert that all frustration must produce aggression or that all aggression stems from frustration. In 1961, for example, Stanford University professor Albert Bandura showed that children who had access to a toy called a Bobo doll would play aggressively and hit the doll when they saw an adult model behave that way but would not play aggressively otherwise.[24] The Bandura study was not a direct test of the frustration-aggression hypothesis, but it did suggest that aggression can be learned. In the book *Roots of Aggression: A Re-examination of the Frustration-Aggression-Hypothesis*, editor Leonard Berkowitz updates but generally supports the Dollard, et al. original hypothesis. Citing studies through the 1960s that showed links between frustration and aggression in various species Berkowitz concluded that "we would have to question those psychologists who *insist* that people have to learn to act aggressively in response to a frustration."[25]

Signs of frustration turned inward

If it is true that Americans are trapped on a treadmill of desire that can never be fulfilled, there should be evidence that people are experiencing more frustration and stress today than in the past and are taking steps to cope with it. Since the brunt of the media onslaught, delayed by the Great Depression and World War II, has taken place since the widespread introduction of television in the 1950s, there should be signs that these changes occurred during the past 60 years or so and were not evident previously. I believe that the signs exist, but like those for global warming the interpretation of them is likely to be controversial.

My starting point is simply to ask: "If people are feeling unhappy, stressed out, and trapped, how are they likely to deal with these feelings?" There might be many answers involving such coping strategies as acupuncture, meditation, religious faith, and exercise, but I suggest that the most appropriate answer is the progression: alcohol or some other form of self-medication, followed next by a visit to the family doctor who may prescribe additional medication, which, if it does not do the job, may lead to some form of psychotherapy.

Self-medication

Human beings have tried just about every conceivable substance to get high from glue to nutmeg, but the most widespread substance used by far is alcohol. It is ancient and widely available. In fact in the 1950s botanist Jonathan Sauer proposed that growing grain for beer was the original basis for civilization. Alcohol use is widespread, almost universal, and it has an especially long history in the United States.

From the founding of the republic alcohol was presented as a component of the good life. Benjamin Franklin is reputed to have said: "Beer is proof that God loves us and wants us to be happy," and apparently a lot of people believed him. In his book *The Alcoholic Republic* historian W. J. Rorabaugh calls the early United States so addicted to alcohol that some leaders feared that it would destroy the new country. In 1821, for example, George Ticknow, a wealthy scholar, warned Thomas Jefferson that if the consumption of alcohol continued for the next 30 years at the rate of the past 30 years the United States would hardly be better than a nation of sots.[26] Rorabaugh suggests several reasons for America's addiction to alcohol one of which was anxiety created by the Industrial Revolution.

It is not necessary here to recount the history of drinking in the 19th century that eventually led to the enactment of Prohibition in the United States in 1919. The Noble Experiment of course was largely a failure and when Repeal came in 1932 America went back to the bottle as one can see readily from movies of the era. Consider the popular series of detective films from the 1930s and 1940s that featured William Powell as *The Thin Man* and Myrna Loy as his wife Nora. Movie reviewer Glenn Erickson has called Nick and Nora's lifestyle the "dream of the Depression's dispossessed." They have a beautiful apartment, wear expensive clothes, and drink all the time "from a room service that's an unending tap." In fact, Erickson considers alcohol to be the most salient thing about Nick and Nora, whom he describes as drinking like fish and being a distiller's fantasy.[27]

According to government sources alcohol consumption in the United States was very high in the early years but leveled off for about a century. From 1850-1950, despite wars, Prohibition, and the Great Depression Americans drank on the average approximately two gallons per person per year. According to US government figures alcohol consumption was 1.98 gallons per person per year on average between 1850 and 1899. (Figure 7.1) In the next 50 years average consumption was 2.07 gallons, a small increase that was not statistically significant. After 1950, however, alcohol consumption rose by more than a third of a gallon per person to approximately 2.35 gallons. That might not sound like a lot but statistically it is significantly more, an increase over the previous 100 years of approximately 15%, and deaths from cirrhosis have increased correspondingly, at least among males.

In 2010 a study by the Organization for Economic cooperation and Development reported that alcohol consumption in the United States had dropped by about 20% to a little less than nine liters of pure alcohol per person per year.[28] Nine liters, however, is approximately 2.4 gallons a figure slightly higher than the 50-year average quoted from US government sources in Figure 7.1. The difference may represent a slight falling off in alcohol consumption by the aging boomer population after the excesses of the 1960s, but it does not change the conclusions of this analysis.

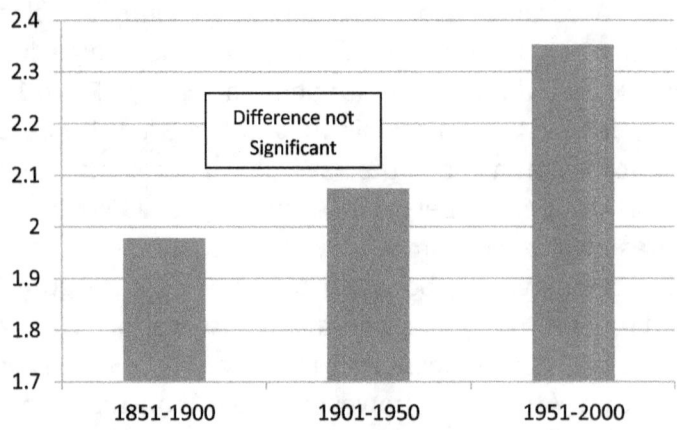

Figure 7.1 Mean Alcohol Consumption in US
(Gallons per Person per Year)

In 2007 a US government funded report found that about 42% of men and about 19% of women reported a history of either alcohol abuse or alcoholism at some point in their lives. Overall, the report concluded, the level of problem drinking is far greater for both men and women than previously believed and much more prevalent and dangerous than society understands.

Prescribed medication

Alcohol may be the most widely used relaxant but it has obvious disadvantages including drunkenness, hangovers, and functional impairment. It is just not a very good substance to use if one wants to cope with the pressures of everyday life and still get some work done. In the 1950s, however, new drugs appeared that offered relief from stress with less impairment of function. Some were used for serious mental and emotional problems such as schizophrenia, but others were prescribed for the general public and soon rivaled alcohol as drugs of abuse. They were the so-called tranquilizers.

Prior to the discovery of tranquilizers there were no good medical options for calming seriously disturbed patients. Until the early 19th century mental illness was known as madness and the mentally ill were either kept locked up at home or confined to asylums that were essentially prisons. Beginning at about 1800 the prisons were replaced by more humane mental hospitals but in the absence of effective treatments these grew into mammoth warehouses some of which held 20,000 or more patients who had little hope of ever recovering and being released. In the early 20th century the only treatments that showed any sign of progress with psychotic patients were the brain operation known as prefrontal lobotomy and electroconvulsive therapy commonly known as shock treatments.

Then a miracle happened. Beginning in the 1950s medications were discovered that calmed the agitated, relieved the depressed, and took away the symptoms of the paranoid. Within two decades most mental hospitals were emptied of long-term patients. Psychiatrists were able to care for the most seriously ill on an out-patient basis by monitoring their medications. The care of less disturbed individuals, from the mildly anxious to the neurotic and depressed fell to general practitioners who had access to an array of new medications and to a host of psychologists and other therapists.

The first drug to be widely used to treat mental illness was chlorpromazine whose anti-psychotic properties were discovered around 1950 in the course of its use as an anesthetic. It is also known as Thorazine.

119

Powerful antipsychotic drugs of this type were sometimes called "major tranquilizers" and have generally not been widely abused by the public. At about the same time that chlorpromazine appeared, however, another class of drug that was originally used to preserve the life of penicillin was found to have calming properties. From this group the drug Meprobamate was synthesized which was given the brand name Miltown and later also marketed as Equanil. Such drugs were sometimes called "minor tranquilizers," and their use and abuse became widespread. By 1957 over 36 million prescriptions had been filled for meprobamate in the United States alone, one billion pills had been manufactured, and it accounted for fully one-third of all prescriptions written by medical doctors.[29]

Other drugs were soon discovered that affected mood and offered hope to the depressed. They not only became widely used but became the basis of a revolution in medical practice that saw general practitioners take over much of the care of emotionally and mentally disturbed individuals from psychiatrists. The breakthrough drug was Prozac (fluoxetine) which first made its appearance in the United States in 1987. A distant relative of the common antihistamine Benadryl, Prozac acts to inhibit the reuptake in the nervous system of the neurotransmitter serotonin making it effective in treating depression and other emotional disorders. More than that, many people believed that Prozac redefined their personalities making them better than they were before, what some called "cosmetic psychopharmacology." In an article in *Newsweek*,[30] one woman exclaimed that "I'm nowhere near perfect, but it is a big, big improvement." Another said: "I call myself Ms. Prozac." Prozac users rapidly became a cult as documented by Peter Kramer's book *Listening to Prozac.*[31] In 2004 doctors in the United States wrote 213 million prescriptions for Prozac and other antidepressants per year.[32] That number increased to 231 million prescriptions in 2006 and 253 million by 2010 making antidepressants the second-most widely prescribed class of medicine in the US after cholesterol-lowering statins.[33] Moreover, almost 75% of these prescriptions are not written by psychiatrists. Other medical experts pointed out the downside of antidepressants including a possible relationship to suicide, but the trend was set. Recent evidence shows that antidepressants are not effective in individuals who are only mildly depressed. According to research performed at the University of Pennsylvania, patients with severe depressions benefit most from antidepressants, whereas those with less severe symptoms see little or no benefit.[34]

With the widespread use of the World Wide Web the distinction between prescribed medications and drugs of abuse has blurred. A Google™ search, for example, for "Prozac prescriptions" yields 2,960,000 links such as the one below. A similar search for "Xanax" prescriptions, an anti-anxiety drug, yields 1,650,000 links. With such medications available to anyone with a credit card it is obvious that no one has any idea what the level of prescription drug abuse is in the United States. Studies show, in fact, that prescription drugs, which can be obtained easily in the home, have become widely abused by teens who view them as safer than street drugs and who sometimes share bowls of random drugs which they call "trail mix."[35]

"Buy Generic *Prozac* Fluoxetine online *Without Prescription.*"

"No *prescription* Needed. Worldwide Deliverly. (sic) Order *Prozac* Fluoxetine online" "*Without* Prescriptions, Cheap *Prozac* Fluoxetine online *Without Prescription.*"

"*Xanax* No *Prescription* Order — Online Drug Shop, Best Prices"
"Cheap online drugs order now visa buy online the best *xanax* no *prescription* paxil MasterCard accepted"

Before the drugs a man or woman who was troubled or depressed and had difficulty coping might spend time talking about his or her problems with a psychotherapist. That kind of therapy is expensive and time-consuming, and insurance companies are less willing to pay for it than they were in the past. It is faster and cheaper, though not necessarily better, for a troubled individual to obtain a prescription from a family doctor so as to acquire what author Ronald Dworkin has called "Artificial Happiness."[36] True contentment in life is more difficult to achieve. As Peter Breggin says: "Depression and love for life are incompatible, and love for life will always triumph when the individual finds the strength and courage to embrace it as the guiding principle of life."[37] That takes time and usually requires help. As millions have learned before now, peace does not come from a bottle — alcohol or pills.

The growth of psychology

The third step in the progression of coping is to seek professional help. The model, of course, is medical practice. Sick people go to the doctor, and that may lead one to believe that doctors have pretty much always done the same thing. The fact is, however, that medical practice has constantly evolved. Two hundred years ago physicians and surgeons could do little more than amputate limbs, lance boils, set bones and comfort the dying. When chemical anesthesia was discovered in 1846 a wide range of surgical procedures became possible. Later in the century discoveries by Pasteur and Koch led to the prevention and treatment of bacterial diseases. Now doctors really had something, and for the next 100 years much of medical practice was devoted to curing diseases. For the most part diseases such as polio and tuberculosis have been conquered, and medical doctors have turned their attention more and more to problems of lifestyle (smoking, obesity) and to aging. These problems were not as important in years past because most people died before they became relevant.

In a similar way psychology has evolved over the years in response to new discoveries and to the ways men and women live their lives. One might think that men and women of the past suffered the same kinds of problems that we do today, but the evidence suggests otherwise. As with medical practice, psychology has also grown in response to social changes. In the late 19th century Sigmund Freud theorized that psychological problems were the result of repressed sexuality. Today there is more openness about sex; the role of women in society has changed dramatically, and from what one sees on television it is hard to believe that anyone today represses anything about sex at all. On the other hand many people today seek help from psychotherapists, including psychologists, psychiatrists, and marriage and family counselors, for anxiety and depression that are related to lifestyle. The curious thing is that psychologists, albeit a different branch that measures and sways public opinion, helped to create the problems.

123

In the early part of the 20th century there were very few psychotherapists, and most people could not afford them. There were only a few thousand psychologists, that is professionals with a masters or doctoral degree in psychology, and many of those worked in academic institutions. Those who worked with the public tended to be diagnosticians who administered tests such as the now discredited Rorschach ink blot test that guided psychiatrists in making treatment decisions. The primary professional group for psychology is the American Psychological Association (APA) founded in 1892. At first it grew slowly. Forty years after its founding it consisted of only about 1000 members.[38] Interest in psychology began to grow in the years leading up to and after World War II, however, so that by 1950 APA membership totaled about 7000. From that point the profession of psychology exploded. By 1980 there were approximately 50,000 members of the APA and by 2010 more than 150,000. The growth rate of psychology in the United States since 1950 has far exceeded the growth rate of the general population. In fact a well known psychologist once extrapolated the exponential growth of the APA based on its rate at the time and whimsically estimated that by the year 2100 it would equal the population of the world.[39]

In his 1970 book *Future Shock* Alvin Toffler predicted that the accelerating pace of life and transience of what he called post-industrial society would result in such signs of breakdown as an increase in drug use, mysticism, nihilism, and vandalism. He attributed these to over-stimulated individuals suffering sensory and informational overload. For Toffler the problem of the future, in which we are now living, would be the speed of life (quantity) rather than its meaning (quality), but speed itself is not the problem. Human beings have adapted to one change after another that increased the pace of life with few signs of maladjustment. In the early 19th century British philosopher and astronomer Dionysus Lardner is alleged to have warned that rail travel at high speed was not possible because passengers, unable to breathe, would die of asphyxia. He was wrong. Very few people chose to move slower when new machines enabled them to go faster, and they did not suffocate. Horse lovers may have lamented the horse's demise but, except for the Amish, no one still uses horses as their primary means of getting around. Similarly, after the discovery of antisepsis by Lister, Koch, and others in the 19th century no one longed for the good old days when a scratch could mean death. The problem with Toffler and more recent futurists is that they see the arms and legs of progress not its soul, circumstance not motives.

A lot has happened over the past 50 or 60 years in the United States including the introduction of oral contraceptives, changes in gender roles and the family, the coming and going of the Cold War, the occurrence of terrorism, economic booms and busts, the invention of the internet, and countless other things. Any and all of these may have added to or subtracted from Americans' sense of well-being. In the end, however, the one thing that has defined who we are and how we feel about ourselves relative to others is our material wealth. Wealth in our society defines success and success is measured in possessions. In that regard I think the deck is stacked against us. The system in which we live, which we have developed in the post-World War II years with the aid of the media, is one that feeds on frustration, and the evidence presented here seems to support that. To help themselves cope Americans drink more than they used to;

use drugs, especially prescription drugs, in huge amounts; and seek help from a system of therapists and support groups that exist in numbers that would have astounded earlier generations. One of the great psychologists of the 20th century suggested a remedy for this American malaise. Carl Jung said: "The goal of life is not and cannot be a continuous improvement of conditions because if conditions become better, the people become worse. The only sensible goal can be the increase of understanding and wisdom. Everything else is bunk."[40]

8. Freedom Revisited

We started with the assertion that the conscious and intelligent manipulation of mass opinion was an important element in democratic society according to Edward Bernays and others because they believed that Americans were too busy, uninformed, or apathetic to care about their role in a democratic society. We saw how that belief coincided with the explosive growth of the mass media after World War I and how the combination of the mass media and the power of suggestion, especially in the young, produced results that could be called truly hypnotic. That fact should have set off alarm bells across the nation, but the majority of Americans, listening intently to their radios, did not hear any. One might scoff and say, after all, that it is just advertising. No one really pays attention to the commercials or political advertisements. They are just of a lot of background noise. If anyone were hypnotizing us or our children we would know and put a stop to it.

During the Hitler era in Germany it was clear from where mass media suggestions were coming and what their purpose was. The Nazi regime controlled the communications media and ruthlessly used propaganda to spread and enforce their doctrines of hatred and militarism. In the post-war United States there was no ministry of commercial information that planned America's consumer economy, and yet an "invisible government" of business and advertising has shaped America's destiny for two generations. In the absence of effective voices exhorting Americans to save money, invest in education, improve health care, repair the decaying infrastructure, and prepare for a world that might be drier and hotter than the present, Americans, goaded on by the media, went on a self-indulgent but unfulfilling spending binge that was only slowed by the Great Recession of 2008-2009. Even worse, our entire society is now geared to keep the consumer juggernaut rolling by means of an educational system that has itself become at worst another aspect of the consumer culture, and at best vocational training for corporate America. Voices that might challenge this system which one used to find in the humanities and the arts are muted if not absent because most Americans simply do not read and are unaware of them. Two questions emerge: (1) what is the harm of somnambulating through a lifetime of media manipulation; and (2) for those who may wish to opt out, what can be done about it?

Life on the meniscus

The result of 60 years of consumerism has been two generations of Americans living on the surface tension of life, the meniscus, like bugs skating on the surface of pond water, never plumbing the depths, perhaps never knowing that there is something below the surface. Far from promoting the ideals of American individualism much touted by conservatives the system produces highly paid technocrats on the one hand, and lower paid "middle class" workers on the other, reminiscent of the social classes in Aldous Huxley's *Brave New World.* In that great warning of the dangers of modernism members of the various classes were indoctrinated nightly during sleep by means of recorded voices that told them that their assigned lot in life was what was best for them. To sop up remaining discontent citizens were given an antidepressant and hallucinogenic drug called soma. In these ways conformity was engineered into the society, and individualism was proscribed. There was no reason for anyone to think because there was nothing to think about.

Some critics of our media-induced consumer culture see parallels with Huxley's dystopia. Our ability to think is becoming increasingly narrowed by the media channels through which we get our information. Contrary views or other perspectives, which one might get through the reading of history and the great stories of humankind, remain nascent in untouched books. It is ironic that electronic books that offer consumers access to hundreds of thousands of titles have become hot selling items. The simple fact is that most adult Americans do not read, and those who do read do not read the kinds of works that prepare one for life in a participatory democracy. According to a 2007 Associated Press-Ipsos poll the average American claimed to have read only four books in the preceding year.[1] Among those who do read, women read more books per year than men by a margin of nine to five, but the poll showed that they primarily read religious works and popular fiction including mysteries and romance novels. Fewer than five percent of readers said that they read books about politics, poetry and classical literature.

Newspapers do not fill the void. Newspaper readership has been declining for more than 40 years. In 1964, for example, approximately 81% of American adults read a newspaper daily. By 2007 that number had dropped to approximately 46%. Some may claim that readers have shifted their source of news and ideas to electronic media. Lol![2] Without a concerted effort to trace down news and analysis on the internet, the twitters and snippets of news one reads among the escapades of starlets, sport stars, and politicians are virtually worthless. The harvest is apparent. In 2008, for example, the Pew Research Center for the People & the Press tested the political knowledge of 3612 American adults by asking three simple questions: (1) Which party at the time controlled the U.S. House of Representatives; (2) who was the current U.S. Secretary of State; and (3) what was the name of the prime minister of Great Britain? The results showed that only 18% of participants answered all three questions correctly. In general well-read participants scored highest but scores for college educated participants were not notably higher than scores for those who had not graduated from college.[3]

Education and American freedom

As Thomas Jefferson said in the Declaration of Independence, "We hold these truths to be self-evident, that all men are created equal, that they are endowed by their Creator with certain unalienable Rights, that among these are Life, Liberty and the pursuit of Happiness." Jefferson's "unalienable Rights" came to be known as the American Dream, a term first coined by writer and historian James Truslow Adams in his book *The Epic of America* (1931).[4] In the book Adams traces the origin of the dream back, before Jefferson's time, to the violence and poverty of Europe. Many immigrants to the New World came with just the clothes on their backs, but their dream was not simply for material goods. According to Adams the dream was for a social order in which each man and woman would be able to attain his or her fullest potential regardless of birth or social position.

The promise of America was more than the life-long pursuit of wealth. It was a promise that hard work would provide a fulfilling life for each individual, but that promise requires wisdom as well as drive. To function as a democratic society Americans need to know how to work with others, engage in civil discourse, and to formulate and express opinions. James Adams, reflecting the views of Ralph Waldo Emerson, believed that Americans needed two kinds of education: one that taught how to make a living ("to have") and one that taught how to live ("to be"). He recognized that many years of study might be needed to master the demands of various careers and professions but, he said, that should not blind us to the fact that learning a trade or a profession was not the same thing as getting a liberal education as a human being. The question is what to teach and how to teach it.

The U.S. State Department, in a document titled *Education and Democracy*, states that education is a universal human right and that school curricula in democracies should include "history, geography, economics, literature, philosophy, law, the arts, social studies, mathematics, and social science courses available to all students – girls and boys." This straight forward statement, however, embodies controversies that have pushed and pulled public education for two centuries. On one side are those who believe that the schools should concentrate on teaching the essentials, such as verbal skills and mathematics, needed to prepare students for the work force. This vocational point of view, emphasizing the learning of facts is sometimes called *essentialism* by educators. An alternative view is that schools should teach things that are of everlasting importance to all people everywhere. Since new facts are constantly being discovered and old ones upgraded, this view stresses the teaching of principles not facts. In teaching science, for example, those who hold this view teach scientific reasoning using famous experiments as examples. In this way students learn that uncertainty and mistakes are part of the discovery process. This view is sometimes called *perennialism.*

Early American education embodied both ideals but focused on essentialism. Most teachers had little pedagogical training and learning was primarily by rote. The typical school was a one-room, ungraded classroom in which children learned reading, writing, and arithmetic. In 1835 the French political thinker and historian Alexis de Tocqueville (1805-1859), initially sent from France to the United States to study the penitentiary system, published the first volume of his famous work *Democracy in America* which included observations on education. Tocqueville noted that Americans were pragmatic and preferred to learn practical subjects "but denounced the metaphysics of medieval scholasticism, Catholicism, and aristocratic education."[5]

From the beginning, however, America's schools also had a second mission: to teach democratic values. Early America was a land not only of promise but also of confidence tricksters, fast deals, and quick exits to the wide open spaces. For educators the future of the republic depended on the teaching of character as well as content. As W. J. Reese pointed out in his book *America's Public Schools,* the formal curriculum was "but a small part of the teaching in a school...the rudiments of feeling [were] taught not less than the rudiments of thinking. The sentiments and passions got more lessons than the intellect."[6] Educators of the day recognized that most jobs did not require a high degree of educational attainment, but for the nation to prosper they did require virtues such as honesty and hard work.

The use of rote memorization and boring teaching methods in schools were criticized by reformers. One was Swiss educator Johann H. Pestalozzi (1746-1827) who said that the role of the educator was to teach children, not subjects. Pestalozzi argued that learning should evolve naturally from observation to consciousness and then to speech. Measurement, writing, reckoning and numbers follow. Pestalozzi, in other words, argued that education should be a process of discovery, of learning how to live as well as making a living.

The ideas of Pestalozzi and other reformers were put into practice in the United States by the founders of progressive education the most prominent of whom was philosopher John Dewey (1859-1952) at the University of Chicago and later at Columbia University. In contrast to traditional pedagogical methods, progressive eduction emphasized learning by doing, group problem solving, emphasis on life-long learning, and education for social responsibility and democracy. Progressive education was widely adopted by American educators in the first half of the 20th century but was criticized by political conservatives during the Cold War era and especially after the launch of the Soviet satellite Sputnik I in 1957. Conservatives disliked progressive education's emphasis on critical thinking, especially in the political realm, and they argued that the unstructured nature of progressivism prevented students from mastering a body of knowledge, especially in the sciences, that was required to maintain

America's technological lead over the rest of the world. Speaking in those days, for example, conservative novelist Ayn Rand called teachers *comprachicos,* roughly "child snatchers" who twisted the minds of the young. The fact is, however, that empirical studies showed that progressive education consistently yielded better results than traditional methods. In the 1930s the Progressive Education Association conducted an eight-year comparison of more than 1500 students in both progressive and traditional programs. When studied at the college level, after having completed the lower grades, students educated by progressive methods did better than traditonally educated students in terms of grades, drop-out rates, intellectual curiosity, extracurricular participation, and resourcefulness. Nevertheless, the resurgence of political conservatism in the Republican victories of the late 20th century reinvigorated the assault on progressiveism and led to the passage of the No Child Left Behind Act.

No Child Left Behind (NCLB) was proposed by President George W. Bush shortly after taking office and signed into law in 2002. It requires each state to set assessment goals in basic skills, primarily reading and math, for all students in certain grades, and a National Assessment of Educational Progress in 2005 revealed marked progress in these areas. Scores for math and reading by nine-year-olds in the three year period after the act was passed were the best in 30 years. Performance gaps between black and white nine-year-olds were reduced and scores for Hispanic students increased. Critics of the act argue, however, that the results are misleading. Setting measureable assessment goals can result in teachers teaching only test problems rather than a deeper understanding of concepts and may encourage states to set their initial assessment goals low so as to maximize improvement. This sort of "gaming the system" apparently happened in Missouri which openly admitted that it had lowered its initial standards.[7]

One of the chief architects of the reforms embodied in NCLB was educational historian and former assistant secretary of education Diane Ravitch who has now completely reversed her position and supports redesigning and strengthening the public system. In her book *The Death and Life of the Great American School System* (2010) Ravitch writes that accountability, as written into federal law, did not actually raise standards but rather dumbed down the schools. She finds United States' educational policies ill-conceived compared with those in nations like Finland and Japan which have the best-performing schools. In those countries, she says, the best college graduates are sought out for teaching positions are paid well and treated with respect. They make sure, she says, "that all their students study the arts, history, literature, geography, civics, foreign languages, the sciences and other subjects. They do this because this is the way to ensure good education." The United States, she says, is on the wrong track.[8]

Religion and American values

Throughout the 19th and early 20th centuries some of the caustic excesses of capitalism in the United States were countered by organized religion, particularly certain Christian denominations, the dominant religion. In the early 19th century various groups, including the Oneida community in New York, the Rappites in Indiana, the

Shakers in New England, and others established utopian communities following commutarian principles. These groups lived separately, away from the problems that were being generated by the Industrial Revolution. Later religious leaders worked within America's slums to ameliorate the terrible conditions they found there. Walter Rauschenbusch, for example, a Baptist minister whose first pastorate was on the edge of New York's impoverished "Hell's Kitchen," developed a theology of Christian socialism that became known as the Social Gospel. It called for the Church to end exploitation, poverty, greed, racial pride, and war.[9] In practical terms, Social Gospel activists established settlement houses to aid immigrants, worked to improve public health, and encouraged better education for poor children. The Social Gospel movement declined after World War II with the decline of mainline Protestant churches although its influence was felt in the Civil Rights movement. Evidence suggests that in recent years some nominally Christian groups have moved away from being the nation's social conscience in favor of the philosophy of success that pervades the broader culture.[10]

Many American Christians endorse a success-oriented mysticism that is antipodal to traditional Christian doctrine. *The Secret,* for example, is a best-selling novel based on a supposed Law of Attraction. This law alleges that there is a universal intelligence that responds to our desires and that as a result our feelings and thoughts can attract events. "The universe, in other words, is a catalog that we can flip through and shop and from which we can surround ourselves with positive people."[11] The idea behind *The Secret* comes from the New Thought movement of the late 19th century with antecedents in the Knights Templar, ancient Egypt, the Rosicrucians, and a 1910 book by Wallace D. Wattles titled *The Science of Getting Rich*.

The Secret continues a long history of success oriented self-help movements that have been allied with American Christianity. One of the first was Christian Science, a religious movement founded in 1879 by Mary Baker Eddy, which asserts that sickness and other adversities exist only in the mind and that they can be overcome by disciplined spiritual thinking. In the early 20th century a French pharmacist named Emile Coué, who discovered that the same medicine worked better if he praised it as he dispensed it to customers than if he did not, promoted the importance of positive thinking with the phrase: "Every day, in every way, I am getting better and better." Since Coué's time many others have advocated the importance of positive thinking and self-help. One of the most prominent positive thinkers was Norman Vincent Peale, longtime pastor of New York's Marble Collegiate Church, whose book *The Power of Positive Thinking* became a national best seller in 1952 and it is still widely read.

Countless books and web sites stress the importance of taking control of one's life and helping oneself to conquer everything from drug addiction to a baseball hitting slump. Many of these are church-related. SuccessChurch.com, for example, offers motivational CDs that include such topics as: "What's Your Marketplace Impact?" "God's Success Entrance," "Developing a Yes & Amen Mindset," and "Your Supernatural Legal Right to Succeed." The same church, based in Troy, Michigan, offers weekly Christian success seminars called "A Richer

Life" which promise to equip one with Biblical strategies and tactics of high achievement for one's life and the marketplace. The SuccessChurch is based on "Christ's Divine Model of Living, High Achieving, and Winning in Life."

Popular televangelist, Joel Osteen, preaches a message of success to 6000 members of his non-denominational Lakewood Church in Houston, Texas and through his weekly broadcasts to seven million viewers in the United States and millions more worldwide in more than 100 countries.[12] He is the author of the book *Your Best Life Now: 7 Steps to Living at Your Full Potential.* Osteen says that he chooses to focus on the goodness of God rather than sin and that he does not include many Bible verses in his books because he sees himself as more of a life coach. Osteen explains that he tries to teach Biblical principles in a simple way, emphasizing the power of love and a positive attitude. Amazon.com lists more than 300 books and CDs under the heading "Christian success" with titles like: *The 7 Keys for Christian Success,* and *Positive Prayers for Financial Blessings.* To many Christians such beliefs are an appalling heresy and nothing more than capitalism with a cross painted on it.

The American Dream revisited

To a larger extent than was true a generation ago both America's schools and religious institutions have become identified with the consumer culture. The result has been to merge the two faces of the American Dream. Personal fulfillment has become identified with economic success, and signs point to that trend continuing. A 2004 poll of American teens conducted by Harris Interactive suggested that contemporary youths hold less materialistic goals than their parents, but a close examination of the results shows that that is not the case. According to the poll: 47% of teen respondents said the American Dream was "simply being happy no matter what I do;" 38% said it was "having a house, cars and a good job;" 30% said "being able to provide for my family;" 27% answered having the "career of my dreams;" 20% said "being rich and or famous;" 7% said "owning my own business;" and 5% said "being the boss."[13]

The results total more than 100% so the teens were obviously allowed to vote for more than one choice. Given that 640 teens were polled, it is possible to calculate the number who chose each option leaving out those who chose "other" or "not sure." Combine the categories of simply being happy and providing for one's family as representing relatively non-materialistic values and combine the rest: house, car, and job; career of one's dreams; being rich or famous; owning a business; and being the boss, as being more materialistic. In this case a clear majority of 56% of teen respondents chose the more materialistic options, which is not surprising given that they have been bombarded from birth with suggestions to consume. Moreover, when asked how much income one would need to achieve their vision of the American Dream 59% said more than $50,000, a figure that was 44% higher than the average per capita income at the time of $34,586,[14] and 41% said they would need an income of $100,000 or more. Today's teens may say that all they want is to be happy, but they know, just as well as their parents, that what they call happiness comes at a high price.

The teens' beliefs about the American Dream are reflected in their choice of undergraduate majors when they go to college. The most popular college major by far in the United States is business. Twenty-two percent of all college degrees are awarded in that field. Fewer than four percent of undergraduates, on the other hand, major in English and only two percent in history. When one considers that only about 28% of the United States' population has completed college, then less than half-of-one-percent of the population has made a formal study of history. The words of philosopher George Santayana that: "Those who cannot remember the past are condemned to repeat it" seem especially ominous. More bachelor's degrees are awarded every year in Parks, Recreation, Leisure, and Fitness Studies than in all foreign languages and literature combined.[15] American students, even at "liberal arts" colleges have largely abandoned the liberal arts.

To some people that term means a patchwork of college requirements that one has to get out of the way before specializing in a career oriented major. Unfortunately colleges foster that view with curricula so diverse and unsystematic that students may graduate without a basic understanding of the great ideas that shape their lives. At one college, for example, science majors were required to take rigorous introductions to the theories and methods of physics, biology, and chemistry but non-science majors could fulfill their science requirement with a disjointed collection of courses affectionately dubbed "rocks, birds, and stars." Such a hodgepodge is not what Adams was talking about when he stressed the need for liberal education. He realized that for a democratic system to function, each man and woman needed to understand history, the law, philosophy, science and religion to make reasoned judgments as a citizen and voter. Horace Mann, a vigorous advocate for public education in the 19th century, said "The whole people must be instructed in the knowledge of their duties...and they must be elevated to a contemplation and comprehension of those great truths on which alone a government like ours can be successfully conducted."[16] The alternative is loss of freedom. If the common man and woman are not well enough educated to govern themselves others will step forward to do the job for them.

In his book *The Five-Year Party* Craig Brandon gives a shocking account of the state of higher education. According to Brandon a vast number of subprime colleges and universities have the retention of students as their highest priority not their education. The result is dumbed-down classes, grade inflation, demoralized professors, luxurious dorms and amenities, and a party atmosphere. Worst of all is the fact that many students leave college burdened with huge loans that will take them decades to pay off. They now realize, Brandon says, their party school education was a kind of scam that promised them lucrative careers which never materialized and left them drowning in debt. There are elite schools, he points out, where academic standards are high, and there may be very good students at poor schools, but for thousands of students perpetual partying is mandatory whereas education is optional. Brandon's assessment is supported by data from the American Institutes for Research which in 2006 reported that most college seniors were unable to understand documents that they might encounter every day, such as a credit card statement, and about 20% were so poor at quantitative thinking that they could not calculate if a car had enough gas to get to a gas station. According to Brandon many educators are alarmed that the illiteracy of American college graduates is a threat to national security. It is not a question of intelligence. Today's young people are as smart as ever. The problem, Brandon says, is one of attitude, motivation, and engagement. "Many young people today," he says, "seem to have lost their motivation to learn and are not afraid of going through life without knowing the basics of how their world, their government, or their economy works."[17]

Those who first settled what would become the United States sought not only to make a better living, they sought to lead a better life. There was no one blueprint for doing that just as there is no one American Dream. There are millions of dreams, each different from the others, and that has always been the case. Not all of the dreams are high-minded. Greed and vulgarity have always been part of the American way of life as have generosity and goodwill. It seems safe to say, however, that somewhere in the 20th century the scales tipped. The balance that Emerson advocated between learning to live and making a living slid perceptibly in the direction of work and wealth. From Puritan preacher John Winthrop's City on a Hill to the Great Seal of the United States that even today places the eye of Providence in every American's purse or pocket, visionaries have held America to a higher standard of conduct than naked self-interest and indulgence. No one could expect their bold outlines to work out in detail, but few would have predicted the dissolution of values in the 21st century epitomized by the demise of Wall Street, and Bernard Madoff's $50 billion Ponzi scheme.

By pursuing an American Dream defined primarily by the consumption of material goods Americans have abrogated the responsibility to educate young people with the values required to maintain our democracy and to preserve it for the future. Part of the blame goes to the "invisible government" of thought manipulators and the media. As we have shown, the effects of media communication can truly be called hypnotic, especially for those who are highly suggestible, but we cannot use that as an excuse. There is no evidence, even in traditional context of hypnosis, that one person can force another to do something against his or her will. Rather, we choose to somnambulate through life, blissfully unaware of the conflicts raging around us, because to do so is easy. Thinking requires effort, and neither our schools nor our religious institutions are equipping young Americans sufficiently to combat the forces of unreason and mass persuasion. Instead, powerful marketing techniques mesmerize Americans into becoming indiscriminate consumers of both products and ideas. Interestingly, critics on the left and the right share the same vision of average Americans, that they are infinitely malleable and capable of being manipulated. The only difference is whether to call them consumers or victims.

There is only a thin line between the ebb and flow of suggestibility in advertising and the ugly reality of political demagoguery. Most advertisements are not vital enough to raise the alarm of totalitarian manipulation, especially in an environment of competing messages. Danger lies, however, in political or commercial messages being transmitted through restricted media filters controlled by powerful and wealthy interests.

We have seen such efforts in political debates where lies and mistruths have replaced open dialogue. On September 14, 2009, for example, conservative critics of the Obama administration staged a "Tea Party" march on Washington. Statistical analyst Nate Silver estimated the crowd to be in range of 70,000. The conservative Fox News Network (FNN), however, castigated the other news media, especially Cable News Network (CNN), for underreporting both the incident and the crowd which (FNN) commentator Glen Beck reported to be 1.7 million. As CNN's Rick Sanchez pointed out on air, however, not only did CNN report the event, but a photograph of the event used by FNN was actually taken by a CNN camera. Moreover, a Tea Party photograph showing a huge crowd, apparently posted by conservative supporters of the march on blogs and Twitter, was a fake. As the Huffington Post reported, the photograph, allegedly taken in September, 2009, did not include the National Museum of the American Indian which opened in 2004. The photograph was apparently taken of the Promise Keepers March in 1997. Moreover, according to Sanchez, the Fox News Network staged its report. In video played on CNN, an FNN producer is clearly seen cueing the crowd around the Fox reporter when to cheer.

In their book *It's Even Worse than It Looks*, T. E. Mann and N. J. Ornstein question whether Fox News qualifies as news. They note that compared to the general population Fox News viewers are significantly less likely to believe that President Obama was born in the United States and are significantly less optimistic about the country's direction. They state that "there is little doubt that Fox News is at least partly responsible for the asymmetric polarization that is now such a prominent feature of U.S. politics."[18]

FNN has been the target of criticism many times for alleged biased and inaccurate reporting. The progressive media watch group Fairness and Accuracy in Reporting (FAIR), for example, stated that during a nineteen-week period in 2001 the ratio of conservative guests to liberals on the show Special Report with Brit Hume was 50 to 6, and that results for other FNN shows were similar.[19] More serious than the accusation of bias is the claim by many that FNN simply lies with regard to "hot button" issues that motivate conservative voters such as abortion. In a June 3, 2009 column, for example, FNN commentator Bill O'Reilly said that he never called murdered abortion doctor George Tiller a "baby killer." That was a lie. According to the website PolitiFact.com, O'Reilly publically referred to the doctor as "Tiller the baby killer" at least 24 times. On June 18, 2009 FNN commentator Glen Beck said that the White House Office of Science and Technology Policy, "has proposed forcing abortions and putting sterilants in the drinking water to control population."[20] This claim was totally false and apparently based on a 1977 textbook that actually rejected such coercive means of birth control. FNN's history of conservative media bias and distortion led Cable Network News (CNN) founder Ted Turner, in an address to the National Association of Television Program Executives, to call Fox News "propaganda" and to equate the network's popularity to Adolf Hitler's rise to power in 1930's Germany.[21]

H. L. Mencken once said: "nobody ever went broke underestimating the intelligence of the American public." The fact is that people are easily misled. In the era of mass communications if people hear or see a statement often enough, no matter how outrageous, many will come to believe it, some fervently. Hitler recognized this fact later called the "Big Lie." Referring to what he believed were Jewish lies about why Germany lost World War I he said:

> Therewith one started out with the very correct assumption that in the size of the lie there is always contained a certain factor of credibility, since the great masses of a people may be more corrupt in the bottom of their hearts than they will be consciously and intentionally bad, therefore with the primitive simplicity of their minds they will more easily fall victims to a great lie than to a small one, since they themselves perhaps also lie sometimes in little things, but would certainly still be too much ashamed of too great lies. Thus such an untruth will not at all enter their heads, and therefore they will be unable to believe in the possibility of the enormous impudence of the most infamous distortion in others; indeed, they may doubt and hesitate even when being enlightened, and they accept any cause at least as nevertheless being true; therefore, just for this reason some part of the most impudent lie will remain and stick; a fact which all lying artists and societies of this world know only too well and therefore also villainously employ.[22]

Hitler's insights on mendacity held a distinguished pedigree. They were anticipated a century earlier by Hortense Beauharnais, step-daughter of the Emperor Napoleon and mother of Napoleon III, who advised her son: "Never tire of claiming that the Emperor was infallible...Assert at all times that he made France prosperous [and] brought to Europe institutions which will never be regretted. If you repeat a thing often enough it will ultimately be believed."[23] Sadly, the Napoleons and Hitlers of the world are right, not because they entrance men and women unwittingly, but because the majority of us are too lazy or ill-informed to tell the difference between truth and a lie so we let others think for us.

In his book *Amusing Ourselves to Death* media critic Neal Postman compares our current state with that of Huxley's *Brave New World.* He believes that we are in a race between education and disaster and wrote continuously about the necessity of our understanding the politics and epistemology of media. "For in the end, he (Huxley) was trying to tell us that what afflicted the people in *Brave New World,* was not that they were laughing instead of thinking, but that they did not know what they were laughing about and why they had stopped thinking."[24]

The antidote to "conscious and intelligent manipulation" is the conscious and intelligent analysis of media messages by informed citizens who understand that material wealth is only one standard for measuring a good life. Democracy takes work. It is founded on the premise that individuals are creators as well as copiers, originators as well as imitators. The job of understanding our world and our place in it cannot be fobbed off on others. It is the job of every man and woman to understand what is going on and to speak out for or against it. This book has been a study of two themes: one of consumerism and material progress, and the other of suggestibility, mass persuasion, and illusory freedom created by media manipulators. They blend into a discordant tune of people lured away from liberty into a pretend world in which the choice of either Coke™ or Pepsi™ seems meaningful. The result is a crisis of our souls in that we seek unimportant things that lie close to the surface because they are pointed out to us constantly by the media. Things of lasting value which are more likely to bring true happiness remain beneath the surface, because no one taught us how to look for them, and we are forgetting that they even matter. It is time to wake up.

Notes and References

Preface

1. Moran, T. F. (1904). *The formation and development of the Constitution.* Philadelphia: George Barrie and Sons, 145.
2. Washington, G. (1786, October 31). *Letter to Henry Lee, Jr.* Alderman Library, University of Virginia. Available On-line: http://gwpapers.virginia.edu/index.html
3. Note: Since the United States was founded 85 electors have voted for someone to whom they were not pledged out of personal interest or by mistake. In 71 other cases electors changed their vote because the candidate to whom they were pledged had died. Available On-line: http://en.wikipedia.org/wiki/Faithless_elector
4. Ellenberger, H. F. (1970). *The discovery of the unconscious: The history and evolution of dynamic psychiatry.* New York: Basic Books, Inc., 528.
5. Ellenberger, H.F. (1970), 528.
6. Tarde, G. (1969). *On communication and social influence: Selected papers.* Chicago: University of Chicago Press, 281.
7. Alterman, E. (2008, March 31). The death and life of the American newspaper. *The New Yorker,* 53.
8. Ewen, S. (1996). *PR: A social history of spin.* New York: Basic Books, 401.
9. Lomborg, B. (2001). *The skeptical environmentalist: Measuring the real state of the world.* Cambridge: Cambridge University Press, 328.

10. Calverton, V.F. (1937, April). Our hypnotized world. *Scribner's Magazine,* 38-42, 89.

1 – The Reality of Hypnosis

1. Hypnotism by radio is latest claim. (1923, July 15). *The New York Times,* 19.
2. Hypnosis by radio has mixed results. (1927, March 10). *The New York Times,* 15.
3. British studio bars television by hypnotist when audition sends judges into trance. (1946, December 21). *The New York Times,* 8.
4. Hypnotism as a defense. (1895, April 8). *The New York Times,* 1.
5. Questions of hypnotism not raised. (1895, April 9). *The New York Times,* 8.
6. Sullivan, R. (1966, December 10). Widow says she saw Coppolino smother colonel. *The New York Times*, 1.

2 – Neither Magnetism nor Sleep

1. Fülöp-Miller, R. (1938). *Triumph over pain* (E. Paul & C. Paul, Trans.). New York: The Literary Guild of America, 28.
2. Tatar, M. M. (1978). *Spellbound: Studies on mesmerism and literature*. Princeton, N. J.: Princeton University Press, 12.
3. Darnton, R. (1968). *Mesmerism and the end of the enlightenment in France*. Cambridge, MA: Harvard University Press, 68.
4. Darnton, R. (1968), 76.

5. Ellenberger, H. (1970) *The discovery of the unconscious: The history and evolution of dynamic psychiatry*. New York: Basic Books, 60.
6. Walmsley, D. M. (1967). *Anton Mesmer*. London: Robert Hale.
7. Darnton, R. (1968), 4, 52.
8. Crabtree, A. (1993). *From Mesmer to Freud: Magnetic sleep and the roots of psychological healing*. New Haven: Yale University Press, 40.
9. Poe, E. A. (1935). *Tales of mystery and imagination*. New York: Weathervane Books, 223.
10. German showman arrested for cutting hypnotized girl. (1928, July 17). *The New York Times,* 12:3.
11. Esdaile, J. (1846). *Mesmerism in India*. London: A. Spottiswoode, 240.
12. Sarbin, T. R. & Slagle, R. W. (1979). Hypnosis and physiological outcomes. In E. Fromm & R. E. Shor (Eds.), *Hypnosis: Developments in research and new perspectives*. New York: Aldine, 273-303.
13. Shepovalnikov, A. N., Tsitseroshin, M. N., Rozhkov, V. P., Galperina, E. I., Zaitseva, L. G., & Shepovalnikov, R. A. (2005). Interregional cortical interactions at different stages of natural sleep and the hypnotic state: EEG evidence. *Human Physiology, 31,* 150-163.
14. Bernstein, M. (1956). *The search for Bridey Murphy*. New York: Lancer Books.
15. Sutphen, D. (1987). *You were born again to be together*. New York: Simon and Schuster Pocket Books.
16. Sugrue, T. (1942). *The story of Edgar Cayce: "There is a river..."* New York: Holt, Rinehart and Winston.
17. Barker, W. J. (1972). The case for Bridey in Ireland. In M. Bernstein, *The search for Bridey Murphy*. New York: Lancer Books, 273.

18. Carroll, R. T. (1994-2009). Bridey Murphy. In *The skeptics dictionary.*
    Available On-line:
    http://www.skepdic.com/bridey.html Visited: April 18, 2010.
19. Barker, W. J. (1972), 272-314.
20. Kline, M. V. (Ed.). (1956). *A scientific report on "The Search for Bridey Murphy."* New York: The Julian Press.
21. Hypnosis expert facing charges on credentials: Psychologist accused of perjury in New York. (1981, Nov. 21). *The New York Times,* 11-13.

3– Hypnotic Susceptibility

1. Harary, K. (1992, March-April). The trouble with hypnosis: Whose power is it, anyway? *Psychology Today, 25,* 56-62.
2. Erickson, M. H. (1964). Pantomime techniques in hypnosis and the implications. *American Journal of Clinical Hypnosis, 7,* 64-70.
3. Bernheim, O. (1917). *Automatisme et suggestion.* Paris: F. Alcan, 47.
4. Weitzenhoffer, A. M. & Hilgard, E. R. (1959). *Stanford hypnotic susceptibility scale: Forms A and B.* Palo Alto, CA: Consulting Psychologists Press.
5. Morgan, A. H., Hilgard, E. R. and Davert, E. C. (1970). The heritability of hypnotic susceptibility of twins: a preliminary report. *Behavior Genetics 1,* 213-224.
6. Haber, R. N. & Haber R. B. (1964). Eidetic imagery: I. Frequency. *Perceptual and Motor Skills, 19,* 131-138.
7. Luhrmann, T. M. (2012). *When God talks back: Understanding the American Evangelical relationship with God.* New York: Knopf.

8. Riddle, W. (2010). Hypnotist hyping a social network mind-control party.
   Available On-line:
   www.switched.com/.../hypnotist-hyping-a-social-network-mind-control-party/ Visited 1/4/2010.
9. Bramwell, J. M. (1930). *Hypnotism: Its history, practice and theory* (3rd ed.). Philadelphia: J. B. Lippincott.
10. Hilgard, E. R. (1965). *Hypnotic susceptibility*. New York: Harcourt, Brace & World.
11. Estabrooks, G. H. (1957). *Hypnotism.* New York: E. P. Dutton.
12. Note. For example, in 2009 Sen. Robert Menendez of New Jersey urged the Federal Reserve Bank to approve an acquisition to save a struggling bank in his state. He did not mention at the time that the bank's chairman and vice chairman were big contributors to his political campaign. Paletta, D. (2010, Feb. 9). Senator prodded Fed to aid ailing bank from home state. *The Wall Street Journal, 1*, 4.
13. Hilgard, E. R. (1965), 287.
14. Schlosser, E. (2001). *Fast food nation.* New York: Harper.
15. Story, M. & French, S. (2004). *International Journal of Behavioral Nutrition and Physical Activity 1*, 3.
16. Gorgias. (2001). "Encomium of Helen." In V. B. Leitch, W. E. Cain, L. A. Finke, B. E. Johnson, J. McGowan, & J. J. Williams (Eds.). *The Norton anthology of theory and criticism.* New York: W. W. Norton, 32.
17. Herrick, J. A. (2001). *The history and theory of rhetoric: An introduction* (2nd ed.). Boston: Allyn and Bacon, 40.

4– Hitler and the Rise of Nazism

1. Shirer, W. L. (1960). *The rise and fall of the Third Reich: A history of Nazi Germany.* New York: Simon and Schuster, 247.
2. Ebert, R. (1994, June 24). The wonderful horrible life of Leni Riefenstahl. *Chicago Sun-Times.*
3. Larson, E. (2011). *In the garden of beasts.* New York: Crown Publishers, 161.
4. Churchill, W. S. (1948). *The gathering storm.* Boston: Houghton Mifflin, 54.
5. Goodman, G. J. W. (1981). The German hyperinflation. Available On-line:
   http://www.pbs.org/wgbh/commandingheights/shared/minitext/ess_germanhyperinflation.html
   Visited: September 1, 2009.
6. Bellow, S. (1987). *More die of heartbreak.* New York: Dell Publishing, 18.
7. Goebbels, J. *The Führer as a speaker.*
   Available On-line:
   http://www.calvin.edu/academic/cas/gpa/ahspeak.htm
   Visited: April 12, 2010.
8. Note: Colgate University has produced a number of outstanding scholars in the field of hypnosis including former President G. B. Cutten, Professors George H. Estabrooks and William E. Edmonston, and graduate John Kihlstrom.
9. Estabrooks, G. H. (1957), 120-121.
10. Hitler, A. (1941). *Mein Kampf.* New York: Reynal & Hitchcock, 852.
11. Goldhagen, D. J. (1996). *Hitler's willing executioners: Ordinary Germans and the Holocaust.* New York: Alfred A. Knopf.

12. Finkelstein, N. G. & Birn, B. R. (1998). *A nation on trial: The Goldhagen thesis and historical truth.* New York: Henry Holt.
13. Milgram, S. (1965). Some conditions of obedience and disobedience to authority. *Human Relations, 18*, 57-76.
14. Milgram, S. (1974). *Obedience to authority.* New York: Harper & Row.

5– Suggestion and the Consumer Economy

1. Rand, A. (2005, ©1943). *The fountainhead.* New York: Plume, 712.
2. Burns, J. (2009). *Goddess of the market: Ayn Rand and the American right.* New York: Oxford University Press.
3. Latourette, K. S. (1953). *A history of Christianity.* New York: Harper and Brothers, 228.
4. Asch, S. E. (1955). Opinions and social pressure. *Scientific American, 193*, 31-35.
5. Shames, M. L. (1981). Hypnotic susceptibility and conformity: On the mediational mechanisms of suggestibility. *Psychological Reports, 49*, 563-566.
6. Graham, K. R. & Greene, L. D. (1981). Hypnotic susceptibility related to an independent measure of compliance: Alumni annual giving. *The International Journal of Clinical and Experimental Hypnosis, 29*, 351-354.
7. Graham, K. R., Marra, L. C., & Rudski, J. M. (2003). Hypnotic susceptibility as a predictor of participation in student activities. *American Journal of Clinical Hypnosis, 46*, 139-145.
8. Graham, K. R. (1980, September 3). *Hypnosis, persuasion and the mass media.* Presidential Address presented to the Division of Psychological Hypnosis at

the 88th Annual Convention of the American Psychological Association, Montreal, Canada.

9. Engles, R. C. M. E., Hermans, R., van Baaren, R. B., Hollenstein, T., & Bot, S. M. Alcohol portrayal on television affects actual drinking behavior. *Alcohol and Alcoholism, 44*, 244-249.

10. Alcohol on TV "prompts drinking." *BBC News*. Available On-line: http://news.bbc.co.uk/2/hi/7921858.stm Visited: April 14, 2010.

11. Bernays, E. L. (1965). *Biography of an idea: Memoirs of public relations counsel Edward L. Bernays*. New York: Simon & Schuster, 386.

12. Phillips, D. P. (1974). The influence of suggestion on suicide: Substantive and theoretical implications of the Werther Effect. *American Sociological Review, 39*, 340-354.

13. Tye, L. (1998). *The father of spin: Edward L. Bernays & the birth of public relations*. New York: Crown Publishers.

14. Graham, K. R., Marchak, F., & Rudnick, A. (1982, October). *Hypnotic susceptibility and cigarette smoking*. Paper presented at the 25th annual scientific meeting of the American Society of Clinical Hypnosis. Denver, CO.

6– The Manufacture of Envy

1. Cohen, B. (1986). *The Snow White syndrome: All about envy*. New York: Macmillan, 41.

2. Morison, S. E. (1965). *The Oxford history of the American people*. New York: Oxford University Press, 761.

3. Morison, S. E. (1965), 743.

4. Roberts, S. (Sep. 14, 2006). Story of the first through Ellis Island is rewritten. *The New York Times.*
5. *Annie Moore memorial fact sheet*. Phoenix, AZ: Irish Cultural and Learning Foundation.
Available On-line:
http://www.azirishmusic.com/Annie_Moore/AMMP_f act_sheel.htm Visited April 6, 2010.
6. Matt, S. J. (2002). *Keeping up with the Joneses: Envy in American consumer society, 1890-1930*. Philadelphia: University of Pennsylvania Press, 1.
7. Matt, S. J. (2002), 4.
8. Untitled. (1926, July 15). *Christian Advocate, 101,* 874.
9. Fromm, E. (1955). *The sane society*. New York: Henry Holt, 108.
10. Schor, J. B. (1998). *The overspent American: Why we want what we don't need*. New York: Harper.
11. René Girard has incorporated mimetic theory in books such as *Violence and the sacred* (1977). Baltimore: Johns Hopkins University Press; and *Things hidden since the foundation of the world: Research undertaken in collaboration with J. M. Oughourlian and G. Lefort.* (1987) Stanford: Stanford University Press; but the following definition, according to Robert Hamerton-Kelly to whom it was dictated, constitutes the first time that Girard explicitly defined his theory.

"The mimetic or imitative theory is an explanation of human behavior and human culture. Human beings imitate one another in everything, including desire. As a result, they choose the same objects and violently compete for them.

Paradoxically, therefore, the same imitative force as brings people together, pulls them apart. The mimetic theory claims that this misunderstood phenomenon is the most important cause of human violence and vengeance.

Vengeance must be the first characteristically human institution. Endlessly contagious vengeance would destroy the species unless some antidote appears. Paradoxically, this antidote originates in the same mimetic impulse as causes the problem in the first place. The mimetic reciprocity of vengeance is randomly deflected upon a single victim which mimetically attracts all violence to itself. This is the process the Greeks called *catharsis,* the *purification* of violence through one solemn sacrificial death. Archaic religion is essentially the ritual repetition of this process in order to renew its efficacy.

Christianity, as modern anthropology correctly points out, is exactly the same schema, with one fundamental difference however, which anthropologists systematically ignore: the attribution of guilt is reversed; the victim is explicitly vindicated.

That is why, far from being one more religion similar to all others, Christianity reveals the lie of all religions, including itself when misunderstood."

12. Wackernagel, M. & Rees, W. (1998). *Our ecological footprint: Reducing human impact on the Earth.* Gabriola Island, BC, Canada: New Society Publishers.
13. Fresh Kills landfill.
    Available On-line:
    http://wiki.answers.com/Q/What_is_the_largest_man_mad e_structure_in_the_world Visited April 6, 2010.

14. U.S. Environmental Protection Agency. (2008, November 13). *Waste-non-hazardous waste–municipal solid waste.*
Available On-line:
http://www.epa.gov/epawaste/nonhaz/municipal/
Visited April 7, 2010.
15. Galbraith, J. K. (1958). *The affluent society.* New York: Mentor, 2.
16. Rogers, E. M. (2003). *Diffusion of innovations* (5th ed.). New York: Free Press.
17. Rogers, E. M. (2003). 35.
18. Gladwell, M. (2006). *The tipping point.* New York: Hachette Book Group.
19. Gaylord, C. & Velasquez-Manoff, M. (2009, Dec. 27-Jan. 3 2010). Horizons: Frontiers of science and technology. *The Christian Science Monitor,* 43.
20. Sweeney, C. (2008, February 28). Never too young for that first pedicure. *The New York Times.*
21. Kohn, S. (2007, August 22). "My Super Sweet 16" and everything that's wrong with America. *CommonDreams.org.*
Available On-line:
http://www.commondreams.org/archive/2007/08/22/
3324 Visited April 7, 2010.
22. Beder, S. (1998). A community view. In Squires, J. & Newlands, T. (Eds.), *Caring for children in the media age: Papers from a national conference.* Sydney: New College Institute for Values Research, 101-111.
23. Wright, J. W. (Ed.). (2007). *The New York Times Almanac.* New York: Penguin.
24. MacMillan, D. (2007, Apr. 16). Big spenders of Second Life: Virtual world residents shell out real dollars for nonexistent clothes, cars, and real estate. Will real-world luxury brands capitalize? *Business Week Online.*

Available On-line:
http://www.businessweek.com/technology/content/a
pr2007/tc20070416_386810.htm Visited: April 12,
2010.

25. Niemi, R. G., Mueller, J., & Smith, T. W. (1989). *Trends in public opinion: A compendium of survey data.* New York: Greenwood Press.

26. Myers, D. G. (1998). *Psychology* (5th ed.). New York: Worth, 410.

27. Russell, B. (1958). *The conquest of happiness.* New York: Liveright Publishing.

28. Rosen, S. (1962). Presbycusis study of a relatively noise-free population in the Sudan. *American Otological Society Transactions, 50,* 135-152.

29. Judt, T. (2008). *Reappraisals: Reflections on the forgotten twentieth century.* New York: The Penguin Press, 394.

30. Graham, K. R. & Clark, M. C. (1969). Psychological pollution. *American Psychologist, 24*, 680-681.

7– The Pathology of Envy

1. Schoeck, H. (1966). *Envy: A theory of social behavior,* (Translated from the German by Michael Glenny and Betty Ross). New York: Harcourt, Brace & World, 348.

2. Mackay, C. (1841). *Extraordinary popular delusions and the madness of crowds.* London: Richard Bentley.

3. Mackay, C. (1841), 55.

4. Milton, J., & Teskey, G. (Ed.). (2004). *Paradise lost (Norton Critical Editions).* New York: W. W. Norton.

5. Cohen, B. (1986). *The Snow White syndrome: All about envy.* New York: Macmillan.

6. Bailie, G. (2001). *Violence unveiled: Humanity at the crossroads*. New York: Crossroad Publishing, 112.

7. Bailie, G. (2001), 113.
8. Available On-line:
   http://en.wikipedia.org/wiki/List_of_wars_and_anthro
   pogenic_disasters_by_death_toll
9. Girard, R. (1977). *Violence and the sacred*. (P. Gregory, Trans.). Baltimore: Johns Hopkins University Press, 240.
10. Salovey, P. (1991). Social comparison process in envy and jealousy. In J. Suls & T. A. Wills (Eds.), *Social comparison: Contemporary theory and research*. Hillsdale, NJ: Lawrence Erlbaum Associates, 261-285.
11. Snow, C. P. (1959). *The two cultures*. Rede lecture presented at the University of Cambridge. Cambridge: UK.
12. Pinker, S. (2011). *The better angels of our nature: Why violence has declined*. New York: Viking Adult.
13. Fromm, E. (1955). *The sane society*. New York: Henry Holt, 15.
14. Marcuse, H. (1964). *One dimensional man*. Boston: Beacon Press, 16.
15. "The war of all against all" first used by Thomas Hobbes in *De Cive* (1642).
16. James, W. (1950). *The principles of psychology*. New York: Dover Publications, 410.
17. McDougall, W. (1923). *Outline of psychology*. New York: Scribner's, 140.
18. Dollard, J., Doob, L. W., Miller, N. E., Mowrer, O. H., & Sears, R. R. (1939). *Frustration and aggression*. New Haven: Yale University Press.
19. Hovland, C. I., & Sears, R. R. (1940). Minor studies of aggression: Correlations of lynchings with economic indices. *Journal of Psychology, 9,* 301-310.
20. Note: The findings of Hovland and Sears have criticized a number of times, most notably by Mintz, A. (1946). A re-examination of correlations between lynchings and

economic indices. *Journal of Abnormal and Social Psychology, 41*, 154-165, but as Reed, et. al. point out: although "a statistical critique by Alexander Mintz cast the reality of the association into doubt...a sample survey of members of the Society for the Psychological Study of Social Issues reveals that Howland and Sears's 'finding' is still widely, if imprecisely, known and accepted." [Reed, J. S., Doss, G. E., & Hurlbert, J. S. Too good to be false: An essay in the folklore of social science. *Sociological Inquiry, 57*, 1-11.].

21. Thomas, D. S. (1925). *Social aspects of the business cycle*. London: Routledge.
22. Marx, K. and Engels, F. *Manifesto of Communist Party.* Chicago: Kerr, 21.
23. Dollard, J., Doob, L. W., Miller, N. E., Mowrer, O. H., & Sears, R. R. (1939), 47.
24. Bandura, A., Ross, D., & Ross, S. A. (1961). Transmission of aggression through imitation of aggressive models. *Journal of Abnormal and Social Psychology 63*, 575-582.
25. Berkowitz, L. (1969). *Roots of aggression: A re-examination of the frustration-aggression hypothesis.* New York: Atherton Press, 5.
26. Rorabaugh, W. J. (1979). *The alcoholic republic: An American tradition*. New York: Oxford University Press.
27. Erickson, G. (2010). The Thin Man on DVD. *TCM Turner classic movies*, Available On-line. http://www.tcm.com/movienews/index/?cid=102329&rss=mrqe Visited: April 20, 2010.
28. Whalen, J. (2010, April 9). U.K. drinking problem gets political. *The Wall Street Journal*, A1, 16.
29. Meprobamate.
Available On-line:
http://en.wikipedia.org/wiki/Meprobamate

Visited: April 20, 2010.

30. Dokoupil, T. (2009, January 22). How mother found her helper. *Newsweek*. Available On-line: http://www.newsweek.com/id/180998. Visited April 20, 2010.

31. Kramer, P. D. (1997). *Listening to Prozac.* New York: Penguin.

32. O'Connor, A. (2004, May 4). Has the romance gone? Was it the drug? *The New York Times*, F8.

33. Wang, S. S. (2011, Aug. 4). Antidepressants given more widely. *The Wall Street Journal.* Available On-line: http://online.wsj.com/article/SB100014240531119038 85604576486294087849246.html

34. Fournier, J. C., DeRubeis, R. J., Hollon, S. D., et al. (2010). Antidepressant drug effects and depression severity: A patient-level meta-analysis. *JAMA, 303*: 47-53.

35. Leinwand, D. (2006, June 12). Prescription drugs find place in teen culture. *USA Today.* Available On-line: http://www.usatoday.com/news/health/2006-06-12-teens-pharm-drugs_x.htm Visited: April 21, 2010.

36. Dworkin, R. W. (2006).

37. Breggin, P. B. (1994). *Talking back to Prozac.* New York: St. Martin's Press, 251.

38. Hilgard, E. R. (1987). *Psychology in America: A historical survey.* New York: Harcourt Brace Jovanovich, 743.

39. Hilgard, E. R. (1987), 744.

40. Allan, J. A. B. and Comment by Samuels, A. (1992). "There is no such thing as a liberal dictatorship: Discovery and first publication of a letter on politics by C. G. Jung. *Journal of Analytical Psychology, 37*, 149-151.

8– Freedom Revisited

1. *The Associated Press*. (2007, August 21). Poll: One in four adults read no books last year.
Available On-line:
http://www.msnbc.msn.com/id/20381678/ns/us_new s-life// Visited: April 21, 2010.
2. Lol! Instant messaging shorthand for "laughed out loud!"
3. *Pew research center for the people & the press* (2008, October 15). Who knows news? What you read or view matters, but not your politics. Available On-line:
http://pewresearch.org/pubs/993/who-knows-news-what-you-read-or-view-matters-but-not-your-politics Visited 3/23/2010.
4. Adams, J. T. (1931). *The epic of America.* Boston: Little, Brown.
5. Reese, W. J. (2005). *America's public schools: From the common school to 'No Child Left Behind.'* Baltimore: The Johns Hopkins University Press, 29.
6. Reese, W. J. (2005), 34.
7. No Child Left Behind Act. Available On-line:
http://en.wikipedia.org/wiki/No_Child_Left_Behind_A ct Visited 3/23/2010.
8. Dillion, S. (2010, Mar. 3). Leading scholar's U-turn on school reform shakes up debate. *The New York Times,* A13, A20.
9. Latourette, K. S. (1953). *A history of Christianity*. New York: Harper & Brothers.
10. *The Barna Group*. (2009, January 12). Christianity is no longer Americans' default faith. Available On-line:
http://www.barna.org/barna-update/article/12-

faithspirituality/15-christianity-is-no-longer-americans-default-faith Visited: April 21, 2010.

11. Byrne, R. (2006). *The secret*. New York: Atria Books.

12. Joel Osteen. (2010). Available On-line: http://en.wikipedia.org/wiki/Joel_Osteen. Visited: April 22, 2010.

13. Hitti, M. (2005). The American dream: Happiness, says teens. Being happy trumps house, cars, and career. *WebMD Health News*. Available On-line: http://www.webmd.com/news/20050113/american-dream-happiness-say-teens Visited: April 22, 2010.

14. Wright, J. D. (2007). Per-capita income by state, 1970-2005. *The New York Times Almanac*. New York: Penguin Group, 325.

15. Menand, L. (2007, May 21). The graduates. *The New Yorker*, 27-28.

16. Messerli, J. (1972). *Horace Mann: A biography*. New York: Alfred A, Knopf, 399.

17. Brandon, C. (2010). *The five-year party*. Dallas: Benbella Books, 71.

18. Mann, T. E. & Ornstein, N. J. (2012). *It's even worse than it looks: How the American constitutional system collided with the new politics of extremism*. New York: Basic Books, 61.

19. *Fox News controversies*. Available On-line: http://en.wikipedia.org/wiki/Fox_News_Channel_controversies
Visited: April 14, 2010.

20. Pitts, L., Jr. (2009, Oct. 4). Beyond ACORN: Fox News lacking. *Bay Area News Group*.

21. *Fox News controversies*.

22. Hitler, A. (1941). *Mein Kampf*. New York: Reynal & Hitchcock, 313.

23. Bierman, J. (1988). *Napoleon III and his carnival empire*. New York: St. Martin's Press, 32.
24. Postman, N. (1985). *Amusing ourselves to death: Public discourse in the age of show business*. New York: Penguin, 163.

Index

167

169

www.ingramcontent.com/pod-product-compliance
Lightning Source LLC
Chambersburg PA
CBHW070903290526
45795CB00001B/223